JUMBLE

SKYSCRAPER

A Superstructure of Peerless Puzzles!

**Henri Arnold,
Bob Lee,
David L. Hoyt,
and Jeff Knurek**

TRIUMPH
B O O K S

For further information, contact:
Triumph Books LLC
814 North Franklin Street
Chicago, Illinois 60610
Phone: (312) 337-0747
www.triumphbooks.com

Printed in U.S.A.

ISBN: 978-1-62937-869-5

Design by Sue Knopf

CONTENTS

JUMBLE®
SKYSCRAPER

Classic
Puzzles

JUMBLE®

Unscramble these four Jumbles, one letter
to each square, to form four ordinary words.

THISO

SUNEE

MENECT

INSLUM

How far you going?

THIS TELLS YOU WHAT
THE FARE IS.

Now arrange the circled letters
to form the surprise answer, as
suggested by the above cartoon.

Print answer here

JUMBLE®

Unscramble these four Jumbles, one letter
to each square, to form four ordinary words.

WHILE
-U-
WAIT

WHAT A GAL WHO'S ON
HER TOES KEEPS.

LEETA

ASTUE

WYIHNN

KOHOED

Now arrange the circled letters
to form the surprise answer, as
suggested by the above cartoon.

Print answer here ⬭⬭⬭⬭ **FROM** ⬭⬭⬭⬭⬭

JUMBLE®

Unscramble these four Jumbles, one letter
to each square, to form four ordinary words.

OMIDI

LEELB

REDOAF

GLUNOE

Brru-therrr!!!

WHAT HE WISHED
HE HAD WORN ON
A BLIND DATE.

Now arrange the circled letters
to form the surprise answer, as
suggested by the above cartoon.

Print answer here **A**

JUMBLE®

Unscramble these four Jumbles, one letter
to each square, to form four ordinary words.

TEJEC

HABIS

RELILK

BONGLE

SOME VETERAN
GARDENERS MIGHT FIND
THIS THE HARDEST
THING TO RAISE.

Now arrange the circled letters
to form the surprise answer, as
suggested by the above cartoon.

Print answer here

JUMBLE®

Unscramble these four Jumbles, one letter
to each square, to form four ordinary words.

LAWZT

ESKOT

HYRITT

RILLAP

A FIGURE IN
THE MIDDLE OF
A FIGURE.

Now arrange the circled letters
to form the surprise answer, as
suggested by the above cartoon.

Print answer here

6

JUMBLE

Unscramble these four Jumbles, one letter
to each square, to form four ordinary words.

LITTE

NOAGY

INGADE

DOMBEY

I'm too good
for them

She never
married

WHAT GIRLS WHO PLAY
HARD TO GET SOME-
TIMES NEVER DO.

Now arrange the circled letters
to form the surprise answer, as
suggested by the above cartoon.

Print answer here ◯◯◯ ◯◯◯

JUMBLE®

Unscramble these four Jumbles, one letter
to each square, to form four ordinary words.

CNOTH

URSOE

SUCCAU

BOAMEA

For her

DO NOT
PICK
FLOWERS

HAVE AN UNHAPPY
EFFECT ON SOME
PEOPLE WITH PLUCK.

Now arrange the circled letters
to form the surprise answer, as
suggested by the above cartoon.

Print answer here

JUMBLE®

Unscramble these four Jumbles, one letter
to each square, to form four ordinary words.

GOGER

MUSIN

LEUXED

TIMCAP

HOW WITCH
DOCTORS KEEP FIT.

Now arrange the circled letters
to form the surprise answer, as
suggested by the above cartoon.

Print answer here THEY "⬡⬡⬡⬡⬡⬡⬡⬡⬡"

9

JUMBLE®

Unscramble these four Jumbles, one letter
to each square, to form four ordinary words.

GUCHO

MUTON

GINKAB

FLIXUN

Sorry, have
to rush

But ...
but ...

SOME GIRLS
BREAK DATES BY
DOING THIS.

Now arrange the circled letters
to form the surprise answer, as
suggested by the above cartoon.

*Print
answer
here* ⬡⬡⬡⬡⬡ ⬡⬡⬡ **WITH THEM**

JUMBLE®

Unscramble these four Jumbles, one letter
to each square, to form four ordinary words.

HACOP

TOODU

RALCOR

SENING

I agree   I agree

WHAT YES-MEN DO.

Now arrange the circled letters
to form the surprise answer, as
suggested by the above cartoon.

*Print
answer
here*

TO

JUMBLE®

Unscramble these four Jumbles, one letter
to each square, to form four ordinary words.

CASEE

ATAGE

UMSCAP

DILVER

COULD BE THE
PRICE OF HIRING
A PRIVATE GUIDE
TO TAKE YOU
MOUNTAIN CLIMBING.

Now arrange the circled letters
to form the surprise answer, as
suggested by the above cartoon.

Print answer here ⟨○○○○○⟩

JUMBLE®

Unscramble these four Jumbles, one letter
to each square, to form four ordinary words.

KREAM

NARFC

INLOOT

RAMPHE

WHAT A CRIMEAN BECAME AFTER RECEIVING HIS CITIZENSHIP PAPERS.

Now arrange the circled letters
to form the surprise answer, as
suggested by the above cartoon.

Print answer here " ⬡⬡⬡⬡⬡⬡⬡⬡ "

JUMBLE®

Unscramble these four Jumbles, one letter
to each square, to form four ordinary words.

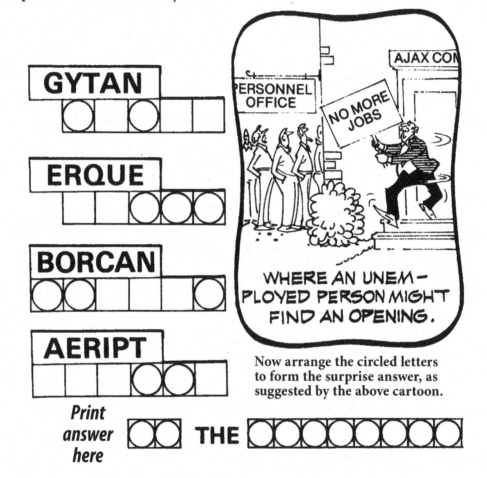

GYTAN

ERQUE

BORCAN

AERIPT

WHERE AN UNEM—
PLOYED PERSON MIGHT
FIND AN OPENING.

Now arrange the circled letters
to form the surprise answer, as
suggested by the above cartoon.

*Print
answer
here* ◯◯ **THE** ◯◯◯◯◯◯◯◯◯

14

JUMBLE®

Unscramble these four Jumbles, one letter
to each square, to form four ordinary words.

REBBI

HOPOW

SLIZZE

PERMAC

WHAT THE POLICE —
WOMAN WHO ENTERED
THE BEAUTY CONTEST
WAS EXPECTED TO DO.

Now arrange the circled letters
to form the surprise answer, as
suggested by the above cartoon.

Print answer here ◯◯◯ A ◯◯◯◯◯

JUMBLE®

Unscramble these four Jumbles, one letter
to each square, to form four ordinary words.

HIWEL

LALIV

WURCEF

GIRDIF

It's outdoors
weather
today

NOT MANY ARE TO BE
SEEN IN THE
CAFE WINDOW.

Now arrange the circled letters
to form the surprise answer, as
suggested by the above cartoon.

Print answer here "☐ ☐☐☐"

JUMBLE®

Unscramble these four Jumbles, one letter
to each square, to form four ordinary words.

LAVIA

PYTEM

GLIJEN

EPSOOP

High-class party

COULD BE THE
RESULT OF A
TOSS-UP—WHAT
YOU SHOULD WEAR.

Now arrange the circled letters
to form the surprise answer, as
suggested by the above cartoon.

Print answer here "◯◯◯◯◯"

JUMBLE®

Unscramble these four Jumbles, one letter
to each square, to form four ordinary words.

HESOW

SUPIO

TREOTT

KUTBEC

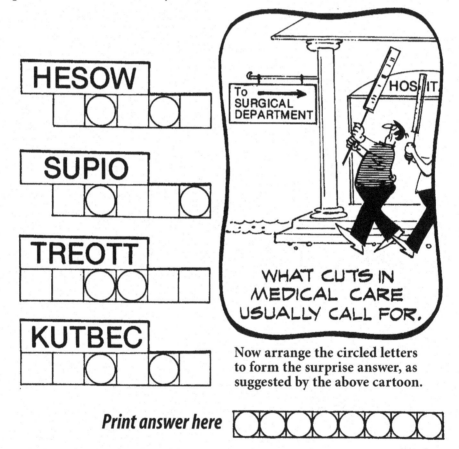

To
SURGICAL
DEPARTMENT

HOSPIT

WHAT CUTS IN
MEDICAL CARE
USUALLY CALL FOR.

Now arrange the circled letters
to form the surprise answer, as
suggested by the above cartoon.

Print answer here

JUMBLE®

Unscramble these four Jumbles, one letter
to each square, to form four ordinary words.

FINEK

VARFO

CHATED

DOHOKE

Lovely apartment

Psst, Dad,
kinda
short
this
month

THE PARENT—
ENDS UP—
PAYING IT.

Now arrange the circled letters
to form the surprise answer, as
suggested by the above cartoon.

Print answer here " ⃝⃝⃝⃝ "

JUMBLE®

Unscramble these four Jumbles, one letter
to each square, to form four ordinary words.

KIHCT

QUSAW

BEIMIB

WHARRO

COULD BE A
QUESTION OF PRICE.

Now arrange the circled letters
to form the surprise answer, as
suggested by the above cartoon.

Print answer here ○○○ ○○○○ ?

JUMBLE®

Unscramble these four Jumbles, one letter
to each square, to form four ordinary words.

DUSEE
◯◯

VOLEN
◯◯

AMBALS
◯◯◯

CLITIE
◯◯◯◯

WHAT HOT MUSIC
DOES TO PEOPLE
WITH "SQUARE" TASTES.

Now arrange the circled letters
to form the surprise answer, as
suggested by the above cartoon.

Print
answer
here

◯◯◯◯◯◯ THEM ◯◯◯◯

21

JUMBLE®

Unscramble these four Jumbles, one letter
to each square, to form four ordinary words.

ENVIL

RASCY

SEAWEL

ABBOOM

Now arrange the circled letters
to form the surprise answer, as
suggested by the above cartoon.

Print answer here " ⬡⬡⬡⬡⬡⬡ "

JUMBLE®

Unscramble these four Jumbles, one letter
to each square, to form four ordinary words.

COAME

MYJUP

LIERIX

ERKLAT

Still at it?

BEAUTY SCHOOL

WHAT THE STUDENT
BEAUTICIAN
HAD TO TAKE.

Now arrange the circled letters
to form the surprise answer, as
suggested by the above cartoon.

Print answer here A ☐☐☐☐☐ - ☐☐ ☐☐☐☐☐

JUMBLE®

Unscramble these four Jumbles, one letter
to each square, to form four ordinary words.

AZERC

MAGDO

NAANAB

RETAIW

WHAT THE DESERT
RAT SAID TO
HIS PAL.

Now arrange the circled letters
to form the surprise answer, as
suggested by the above cartoon.

Print
answer
here

⬡⬡⬡⬡⬡ WE ⬡⬡⬡⬡⬡ DO?

JUMBLE®

Unscramble these four Jumbles, one letter
to each square, to form four ordinary words.

PUPER

WHART

CENNAD

LEWBIA

Guilty!

DID THE LAWYER
DO HIS BEST
IN COURT?

Now arrange the circled letters
to form the surprise answer, as
suggested by the above cartoon.

Print answer here ⬡⬡ " ⬡⬡⬡⬡⬡ "

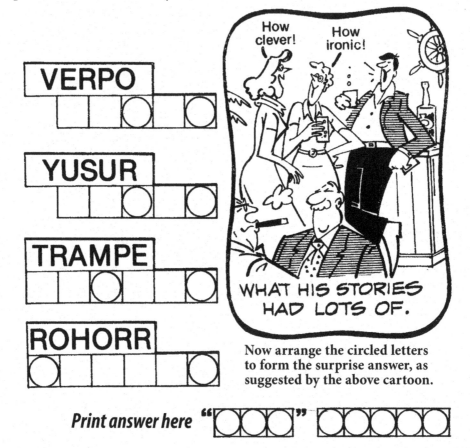

JUMBLE®

Unscramble these four Jumbles, one letter
to each square, to form four ordinary words.

VERPO

YUSUR

TRAMPE

ROHORR

How
clever!

How
ironic!

WHAT HIS STORIES
HAD LOTS OF.

Now arrange the circled letters
to form the surprise answer, as
suggested by the above cartoon.

Print answer here " ☐☐☐ " ☐☐☐☐☐

JUMBLE®
SKYSCRAPER

Daily Puzzles

JUMBLE®

Unscramble these four Jumbles, one letter
to each square, to form four ordinary words.

TYIED

YATHS

ENBARN

GAIWHE

WHAT THEY HAD TO
DO WHEN THE CLOCK
COLLECTOR PASSED
AWAY.

Now arrange the circled letters
to form the surprise answer, as
suggested by the above cartoon.

**Print
answer
here** ☐☐☐☐☐ UP HIS ☐☐☐☐☐☐☐

28

JUMBLE®

Unscramble these four Jumbles, one letter
to each square, to form four ordinary words.

LAGED

WAMAC

ROLARP

YONDOB

TRY THIS DIET
IF YOU WANT TO
BECOME A TIGHT-
ROPE WALKER.

Now arrange the circled letters
to form the surprise answer, as
suggested by the above cartoon.

Print answer here " ⬡⬡⬡⬡⬡⬡⬡⬡ "

JUMBLE®

Unscramble these four Jumbles, one letter
to each square, to form four ordinary words.

YOANG

POTEM

VINNET

CAMIOT

WHAT THE TRUMPET
PLAYER'S GIRL
FRIEND ACCUSED
HIM OF DOING.

Now arrange the circled letters
to form the surprise answer, as
suggested by the above cartoon.

*Print
answer
here*

☐☐☐☐ – ☐☐☐☐☐☐ HER

JUMBLE®

Unscramble these four Jumbles, one letter
to each square, to form four ordinary words.

TROFY

DUTEE

NORGAD

VORGEN

WHAT HE SAID
WHEN ASKED
WHETHER HE HAD
LIKED COLLEGE.

Now arrange the circled letters
to form the surprise answer, as
suggested by the above cartoon.

Print answer here ☐☐ A "☐☐☐☐☐☐"

31

JUMBLE®

Unscramble these four Jumbles, one letter
to each square, to form four ordinary words.

YONAN

GUDOH

LOICAS

RUINJY

MIGHT DESCRIBE
SOME THINGS DONE
IN CONGRESS.

Now arrange the circled letters
to form the surprise answer, as
suggested by the above cartoon.

**Print answer
here** " ◯◯◯◯◯◯◯◯◯◯◯◯ "

JUMBLE®

Unscramble these four Jumbles, one letter
to each square, to form four ordinary words.

RILLT

YADDD

WHOALL

FADGYL

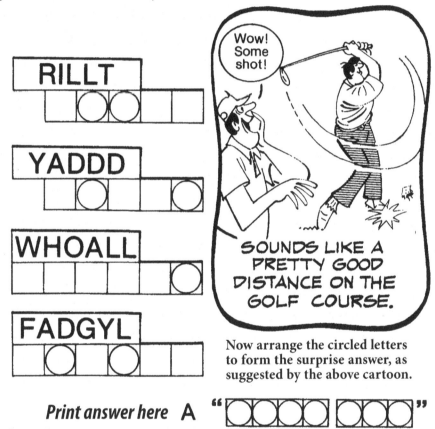

Wow!
Some
shot!

SOUNDS LIKE A
PRETTY GOOD
DISTANCE ON THE
GOLF COURSE.

Now arrange the circled letters
to form the surprise answer, as
suggested by the above cartoon.

Print answer here A " ☐☐☐☐ ☐☐☐ "

JUMBLE®

Unscramble these four Jumbles, one letter
to each square, to form four ordinary words.

YAHIR

DEVEL

SOXEEP

HOCCUR

"HERE'S HOW!" —
IN THE KITCHEN.

Now arrange the circled letters
to form the surprise answer, as
suggested by the above cartoon.

Print answer here

JUMBLE.

Unscramble these four Jumbles, one letter
to each square, to form four ordinary words.

YODIL

AVVLE

VILEWE

INNACE

JUST
MAR

WORDS HEARD
DURING A
HONEYMOON.

Now arrange the circled letters
to form the surprise answer, as
suggested by the above cartoon.

Print answer here "⬚ ⬚⬚⬚⬚ ⬚⬚⬚⬚"

JUMBLE®

Unscramble these four Jumbles, one letter to each square, to form four ordinary words.

HORAC

YALLD

PLAICH

GREEME

REPRESENTS THE COUNTRY — ON PAPER, AT LEAST.

Now arrange the circled letters to form the surprise answer, as suggested by the above cartoon.

Print answer here ◯ ◯◯◯

JUMBLE®

Unscramble these four Jumbles, one letter
to each square, to form four ordinary words.

PHACT

DRUIL

KEENAW

RETINE

How much
longer?

WHAT A MODEL
MAY BE WHEN
UNDER A STRAIN.

Now arrange the circled letters
to form the surprise answer, as
suggested by the above cartoon.

Print answer here " ◯◯◯◯◯ "

JUMBLE ®

Unscramble these four Jumbles, one letter
to each square, to form four ordinary words.

JEDDA

CRAHN

DERAIM

PIDUST

HOW TO CONSTRUCT
AN "INDUSTRY"
OUT OF NUDITY.

Now arrange the circled letters
to form the surprise answer, as
suggested by the above cartoon.

Print answer here

JUMBLE®

Unscramble these four Jumbles, one letter
to each square, to form four ordinary words.

LAGIE

OUMES

SIPCLE

AINNIZ

WHAT A GOOD
CLOTHING SALESMAN
DOES WITH A
NEW CUSTOMER.

Now arrange the circled letters
to form the surprise answer, as
suggested by the above cartoon.

Print answer here ◯◯◯◯◯ HIM ◯◯

JUMBLE®

Unscramble these four Jumbles, one letter
to each square, to form four ordinary words.

LIWLT

YUTIN

FAHBLE

GULJEG

Nothing to worry about

WHAT THEY MADE
WHEN THERE WAS A
POWER FAILURE.

Now arrange the circled letters
to form the surprise answer, as
suggested by the above cartoon.

Print answer here ⬡⬡⬡⬡⬡ OF ⬡⬡

JUMBLE®

Unscramble these four Jumbles, one letter to each square, to form four ordinary words.

YERAW

FYLOT

ERVEWS

NIRBON

London tomorrow ... next, Paris ... then back to the Met

FOR THESE OPERA SINGERS—COULD BE NO REST.

Now arrange the circled letters to form the surprise answer, as suggested by the above cartoon.

Print answer here " ◯◯◯◯◯◯◯ "

JUMBLE®

Unscramble these four Jumbles, one letter
to each square, to form four ordinary words.

POZAT

KANLY

DANAGE

MOFTEN

Well ...maybe ... if ...???

ADD SOMETHING TO
A "NO," AND IT
MIGHT BE YES.

Now arrange the circled letters
to form the surprise answer, as
suggested by the above cartoon.

Print answer here ☐ "☐☐-☐"

42

JUMBLE®

Unscramble these four Jumbles, one letter
to each square, to form four ordinary words.

YAMOF

NIYKK

TURAIN

REOCAN

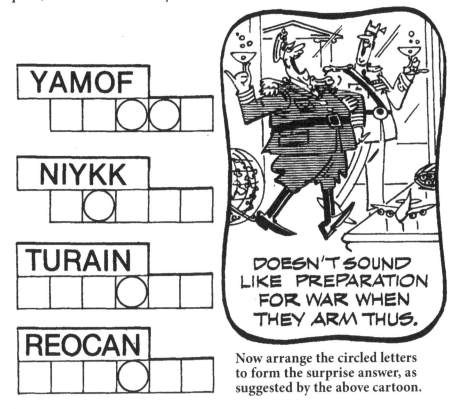

DOESN'T SOUND
LIKE PREPARATION
FOR WAR WHEN
THEY ARM THUS.

Now arrange the circled letters
to form the surprise answer, as
suggested by the above cartoon.

Print answer here " ☐☐ ☐☐☐ "

JUMBLE®

Unscramble these four Jumbles, one letter
to each square, to form four ordinary words.

LALAM

YAASS

NATFUL

CHELEK

GA GA

WHAT LITTLE BABIES
SOMETIMES
INDULGE IN.

Now arrange the circled letters
to form the surprise answer, as
suggested by the above cartoon.

Print answer here "⬡⬡⬡⬡⬡" ⬡⬡⬡⬡

JUMBLE

Unscramble these four Jumbles, one letter
to each square, to form four ordinary words.

WYLLO

FASHE

LAYGEL

TIENIF

Revenooers!

A KIND OF "ART"
YOU MIGHT BE SUR-
PRISED TO FIND IN
A MOVING PICTURE.

Now arrange the circled letters
to form the surprise answer, as
suggested by the above cartoon.

Print answer here " ⬡⬡⬡⬡⬡ " ⬡⬡⬡⬡

JUMBLE®

Unscramble these four Jumbles, one letter
to each square, to form four ordinary words.

TOINX

LEETA

RAFTLE

MAIDDY

IF AN ALTERATION
IS REQUIRED, YOU
SHOULD GET IT
FROM THIS.

Now arrange the circled letters
to form the surprise answer, as
suggested by the above cartoon.

Print answer
here

A " ⃝⃝⃝⃝ ⃝⃝⃝⃝⃝⃝ "

JUMBLE®

Unscramble these four Jumbles, one letter
to each square, to form four ordinary words.

IKKAH

UPDYM

ANSTUE

NITTEY

WHAT THE CAPTAIN
OF THE ARK SAID
HE HAD NO
SHORTAGE OF.

Now arrange the circled letters
to form the surprise answer, as
suggested by the above cartoon.

Print answer here " ◯◯◯◯◯ "

JUMBLE®

Unscramble these four Jumbles, one letter
to each square, to form four ordinary words.

TAGUM

SWEHL

DEPHUL

SLAQUL

A VERY FINE WOOD
WAS IN EVIDENCE.

Now arrange the circled letters
to form the surprise answer, as
suggested by the above cartoon.

Print answer here

JUMBLE®

Unscramble these four Jumbles, one letter
to each square, to form four ordinary words.

YAWNT

DYKEE

ROUGAC

BINNGE

I HAVE A CERTAIN
IMPORTANCE WHEN ANGRY!

Don't they
know who
I am?

Now arrange the circled letters
to form the surprise answer, as
suggested by the above cartoon.

Print answer here "◯ - ◯◯◯◯"

49

JUMBLE®

Unscramble these four Jumbles, one letter
to each square, to form four ordinary words.

HAWSS

FONTE

REFOLG

YAFULT

It's all yours!

GENERALLY LEFT
AT THE SINK.

Now arrange the circled letters
to form the surprise answer, as
suggested by the above cartoon.

Print answer here THE ⬡⬡⬡ ⬡⬡⬡⬡⬡

JUMBLE®

Unscramble these four Jumbles, one letter
to each square, to form four ordinary words.

TEFAC

KULCC

OBNIBB

NYGERT

INCLINED TO BE ON
THE THIN SIDE.

Now arrange the circled letters
to form the surprise answer, as
suggested by the above cartoon.

Print answer here

JUMBLE®

Unscramble these four Jumbles, one letter
to each square, to form four ordinary words.

RAMER

TABBO

BLUJEM

CAVIDE

You're late for the game!

Washout by the river

CRASH!

A BRIDGE FOUNDATION THAT MAY COLLAPSE.

Now arrange the circled letters
to form the surprise answer, as
suggested by the above cartoon.

Print answer here A ⬡⬡⬡⬡⬡ ⬡⬡⬡⬡⬡

JUMBLE®

Unscramble these four Jumbles, one letter
to each square, to form four ordinary words.

VENOW

REIND

VOALAW

DILBER

HOW THE PLUMBER
FELT AFTER A
HARD DAY'S WORK.

Now arrange the circled letters
to form the surprise answer, as
suggested by the above cartoon.

Print answer here " "

JUMBLE®

Unscramble these four Jumbles, one letter
to each square, to form four ordinary words.

ALYMN

URSOE

NATTEX

TIPEOA

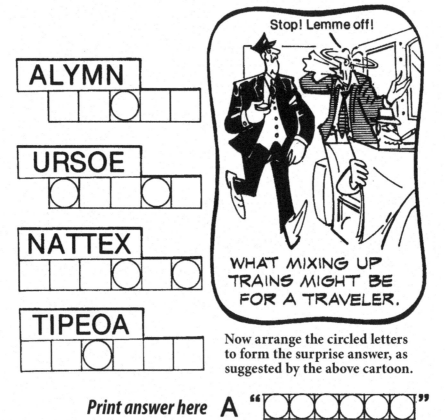

Stop! Lemme off!

WHAT MIXING UP
TRAINS MIGHT BE
FOR A TRAVELER.

Now arrange the circled letters
to form the surprise answer, as
suggested by the above cartoon.

Print answer here A " ◯◯◯◯◯◯◯ "

JUMBLE®

Unscramble these four Jumbles, one letter
to each square, to form four ordinary words.

BYRIN

DIXEO

REPHOG

FEYGIF

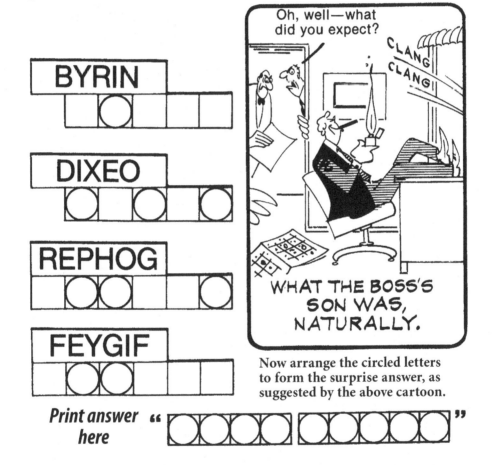

Oh, well—what
did you expect?

CLANG
CLANG

WHAT THE BOSS'S
SON WAS,
NATURALLY.

Now arrange the circled letters
to form the surprise answer, as
suggested by the above cartoon.

Print answer here " ☐☐☐☐ ☐☐☐☐☐ "

JUMBLE®

Unscramble these four Jumbles, one letter to each square, to form four ordinary words.

GUFED

LULET

CRONAR

INPYGA

Guess he's having too much fun as a bachelor

WHAT SOME GUYS WHO NEVER SEEM TO GET AROUND TO MARRYING JUST GET.

Now arrange the circled letters to form the surprise answer, as suggested by the above cartoon.

Print answer here " "

JUMBLE®

Unscramble these four Jumbles, one letter to each square, to form four ordinary words.

CHAVO

INGAR

JENTIC

YURSLE

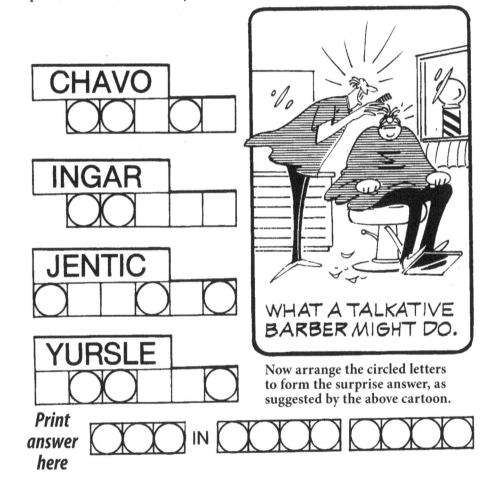

WHAT A TALKATIVE BARBER MIGHT DO.

Now arrange the circled letters to form the surprise answer, as suggested by the above cartoon.

Print answer here ☐☐☐ IN ☐☐☐☐☐ ☐☐☐☐

57

JUMBLE®

Unscramble these four Jumbles, one letter
to each square, to form four ordinary words.

SUHOE

FARIE

TRENGY

PINDAK

He doesn't have any
real authority

WHAT THE CHAIRMAN
OF THE MATHEMATICS
DEPARTMENT WAS
CALLED.

Now arrange the circled letters
to form the surprise answer, as
suggested by the above cartoon.

**Print answer
here** THE ◯◯◯◯◯◯◯◯◯◯◯

JUMBLE®

Unscramble these four Jumbles, one letter
to each square, to form four ordinary words.

RUGAU

OTTOH

NYWIRT

CARILA

WHAT THE PATIENT
SAID WHEN HIS
DOCTOR TOLD HIM
TO DIET.

Now arrange the circled letters
to form the surprise answer, as
suggested by the above cartoon.

*Print answer
here*

◯◯◯◯ ◯◯◯◯◯ **?**

JUMBLE®

Unscramble these four Jumbles, one letter
to each square, to form four ordinary words.

YILCI

KARCC

DAMMAN

TARGEY

WHEN THEY TOOK THAT
TROPICAL VACATION,
THEY APPARENTLY
WERE SAVING THEIR
MONEY FOR THIS.

Now arrange the circled letters
to form the surprise answer, as
suggested by the above cartoon.

Print answer here A ⬡⬡⬡⬡⬡ ⬡⬡⬡

JUMBLE®

Unscramble these four Jumbles, one letter to each square, to form four ordinary words.

THEFC

CHITH

TELTAC

RAYPOD

Next!

WHAT THEY CALLED THE TEAM'S PSYCHIATRIST.

Now arrange the circled letters to form the surprise answer, as suggested by the above cartoon.

Print answer here   THE " ◯◯◯◯◯ " ◯◯◯◯◯

JUMBLE®

Unscramble these four Jumbles, one letter
to each square, to form four ordinary words.

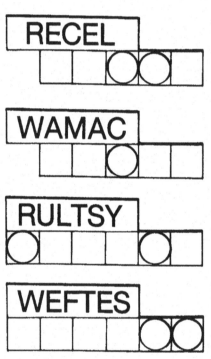

RECEL

WAMAC

RULTSY

WEFTES

ALCOHOL WILL
PRESERVE ALMOST
EVERYTHING
EXCEPT THIS.

Now arrange the circled letters
to form the surprise answer, as
suggested by the above cartoon.

Print answer here

JUMBLE®

Unscramble these four Jumbles, one letter
to each square, to form four ordinary words.

CANKK

PUTIL

ZOLENZ

WHACES

WHAT SOME PEOPLE
DO AT SNEAK
PREVIEWS.

Now arrange the circled letters
to form the surprise answer, as
suggested by the above cartoon.

Print answer here

JUMBLE®

Unscramble these four Jumbles, one letter
to each square, to form four ordinary words.

DYKEE

CIROU

RYVETS

WALCOL

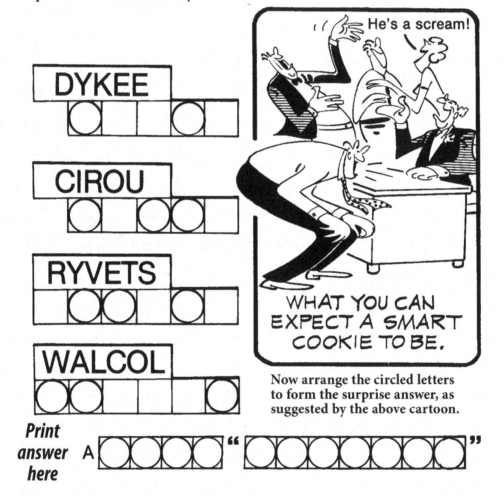

He's a scream!

WHAT YOU CAN
EXPECT A SMART
COOKIE TO BE.

Now arrange the circled letters
to form the surprise answer, as
suggested by the above cartoon.

Print
answer
here

A ⃝⃝⃝⃝ " ⃝⃝⃝⃝⃝⃝⃝ "

JUMBLE®

Unscramble these four Jumbles, one letter
to each square, to form four ordinary words.

YOOBT

DUMIO

ORTETT

GUMPSY

Brother—can you spare
a dime?

IF IT'S DRACULA WHOM
YOU MEET ON THE
STREET, HE'LL SURE
KNOW HOW TO
DO THIS.

Now arrange the circled letters
to form the surprise answer, as
suggested by the above cartoon.

Print
answer
here

⬡⬡⬡ THE ⬡⬡⬡⬡⬡ ON ⬡⬡⬡

JUMBLE®

Unscramble these four Jumbles, one letter to each square, to form four ordinary words.

ISTUE

TASHY

PRUMAK

MASTIG

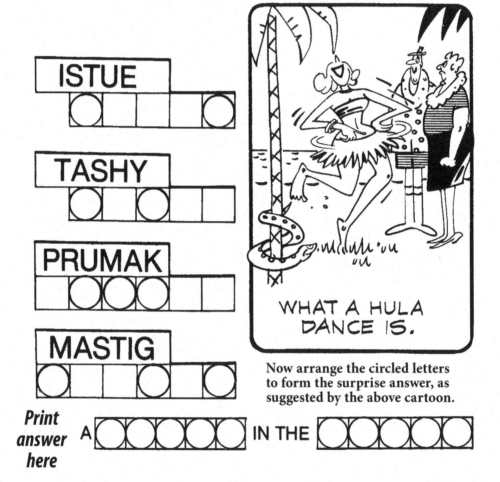

WHAT A HULA
DANCE IS.

Now arrange the circled letters to form the surprise answer, as suggested by the above cartoon.

Print answer here

A ⬡⬡⬡⬡⬡ IN THE ⬡⬡⬡⬡⬡

JUMBLE®

Unscramble these four Jumbles, one letter
to each square, to form four ordinary words.

TARAP

CAPHO

POAFFY

HEERCY

WHAT THEY CALLED
THE POLICE
OFFICERS' ANNUAL
SHINDIG.

Now arrange the circled letters
to form the surprise answer, as
suggested by the above cartoon.

Print answer here   THE " ◯◯◯ ◯◯◯ "

JUMBLE®

Unscramble these four Jumbles, one letter
to each square, to form four ordinary words.

PROAN

DAHYN

MEENZY

ZARABA

WHAT THE
PICNICKERS WERE.

Now arrange the circled letters
to form the surprise answer, as
suggested by the above cartoon.

Print answer here " ◯◯◯◯◯◯◯◯ "

JUMBLE®

Unscramble these four Jumbles, one letter
to each square, to form four ordinary words.

NINOO

CNATH

STEGAK

STELEN

CLANG

WHERE THERE'S
SMOKE —

Now arrange the circled letters
to form the surprise answer, as
suggested by the above cartoon.

*Print
answer
here*

JUMBLE®

Unscramble these four Jumbles, one letter
to each square, to form four ordinary words.

MUIBE

SULLK

DACLUN

MYSLOB

CONCER
TONITE

WHAT THE GUY
WHOSE SHOES
SQUEAKED
MUST HAVE HAD.

Now arrange the circled letters
to form the surprise answer, as
suggested by the above cartoon.

Print
answer
here   ⬚⬚⬚⬚⬚ IN HIS " ⬚⬚⬚⬚ "

JUMBLE®

Unscramble these four Jumbles, one letter
to each square, to form four ordinary words.

TYJET

YARIN

RODIAT

VEELAC

WHAT THE
BALLERINA
INSISTED THAT
HER PARTNER DO.

Now arrange the circled letters
to form the surprise answer, as
suggested by the above cartoon.

Print answer here " ◯◯◯ " THE ◯◯◯◯

JUMBLE®

Unscramble these four Jumbles, one letter
to each square, to form four ordinary words.

TINJO

BICCU

ROCCEE

SIMYAD

THERE'S PLENTY OF
THIS WHEN A MAN
DOESN'T PAY
ALIMONY.

Now arrange the circled letters
to form the surprise answer, as
suggested by the above cartoon.

Print answer here

72

JUMBLE

Unscramble these four Jumbles, one letter
to each square, to form four ordinary words.

NAHVE

KWATE

YOPMIC

YALAWY

VAN SNOOT AND CO.

THE BOSS ALWAYS
CAME IN EARLY TO
SEE THIS.

Now arrange the circled letters
to form the surprise answer, as
suggested by the above cartoon.

Print
answer
here

IN

JUMBLE®

Unscramble these four Jumbles, one letter
to each square, to form four ordinary words.

NABOR
◯◯□□◯

TEWCI
□□◯□□

WEDDEG
□□□◯◯□

FALLUW
◯□□□◯◯

He's always botching things up

WHAT THAT
INCOMPETENT
POLITICIAN
SEEMED TO LIVE BY.

Now arrange the circled letters
to form the surprise answer, as
suggested by the above cartoon.

Print
answer THE ◯◯◯ OF THE "◯◯◯◯◯◯"
here

74

JUMBLE®

Unscramble these four Jumbles, one letter
to each square, to form four ordinary words.

YETTS
⬜◯◯◯⬜

DEBIA
⬜◯⬜⬜⬜

LIERIX
◯◯⬜⬜⬜◯

NIGLAC
◯◯◯⬜⬜⬜

IN ORDER TO SELECT
THE FINEST WINE,
EXAMINE THIS.

Now arrange the circled letters
to form the surprise answer, as
suggested by the above cartoon.

*Print
answer
here* THE ◯◯◯◯◯ - ◯◯◯◯◯◯◯ LIST

JUMBLE®

Unscramble these four Jumbles, one letter
to each square, to form four ordinary words.

DUGEN

KNARC

DERAIV

ROVACT

WHEN YOU'RE IN IT,
YOU NEVER KNOW.

Now arrange the circled letters
to form the surprise answer, as
suggested by the above cartoon.

Print answer here

JUMBLE®

Unscramble these four Jumbles, one letter
to each square, to form four ordinary words.

VERBA

ONLOY

SLAVAS

MUCPIE

NO TALKING

Shh!

Shh!

WHAT THE POLITE
CROOK USED WHEN
HE HELD UP THE
PUBLIC LIBRARY.

Now arrange the circled letters
to form the surprise answer, as
suggested by the above cartoon.

Print answer here A ◯◯◯◯◯◯◯◯◯

JUMBLE®

Unscramble these four Jumbles, one letter
to each square, to form four ordinary words.

LIEBE

YURLT

KEWRAH

EVITLY

SOME PEOPLE WHO
THINK THEY'RE "IN
THE SWIM" ARE
JUST THIS.

Now arrange the circled letters
to form the surprise answer, as
suggested by the above cartoon.

Print answer here ☐☐☐ ☐☐☐

JUMBLE®

Unscramble these four Jumbles, one letter to each square, to form four ordinary words.

UDGIE

ENVOW

NITTEY

VOCLEN

MY HUSBAND FOUND A NEW POSITION—

RACING

Now arrange the circled letters to form the surprise answer, as suggested by the above cartoon.

Print answer here " ◯◯◯◯◯◯ ◯◯◯◯ "

JUMBLE®

Unscramble these four Jumbles, one letter
to each square, to form four ordinary words.

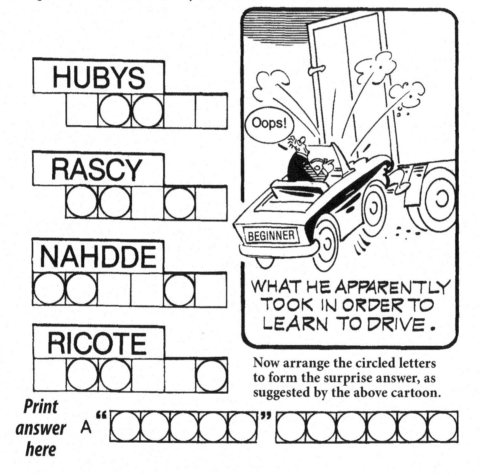

HUBYS

RASCY

NAHDDE

RICOTE

WHAT HE APPARENTLY
TOOK IN ORDER TO
LEARN TO DRIVE.

Now arrange the circled letters
to form the surprise answer, as
suggested by the above cartoon.

Print
answer A "⬡⬡⬡⬡⬡" ⬡⬡⬡⬡⬡⬡
here

JUMBLE®

Unscramble these four Jumbles, one letter
to each square, to form four ordinary words.

ZUZYF

LUKKS

RODAFE

ETTIPE

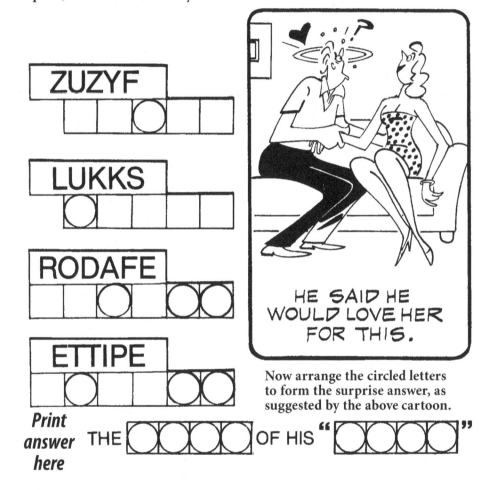

HE SAID HE
WOULD LOVE HER
FOR THIS.

Now arrange the circled letters
to form the surprise answer, as
suggested by the above cartoon.

*Print
answer
here* THE ⬡⬡⬡⬡ OF HIS "⬡⬡⬡⬡"

JUMBLE®

Unscramble these four Jumbles, one letter
to each square, to form four ordinary words.

LERBY

MUGMY

ENVARG

VORPLE

HOW TO ACQUIRE
A HUGE
VOCABULARY.

Now arrange the circled letters
to form the surprise answer, as
suggested by the above cartoon.

Print answer here ○○○○○○ ○○○

JUMBLE®

Unscramble these four Jumbles, one letter
to each square, to form four ordinary words.

WRONC

FARET

NERYTD

GAROFE

THE RODENT WHO LIVED IN
THE BIG CITY WAS GROWING
TIRED OF THE ---

Now arrange the circled letters
to form the surprise answer, as
suggested by the above cartoon.

Print answer here

JUMBLE®

Unscramble these four Jumbles, one letter to each square, to form four ordinary words.

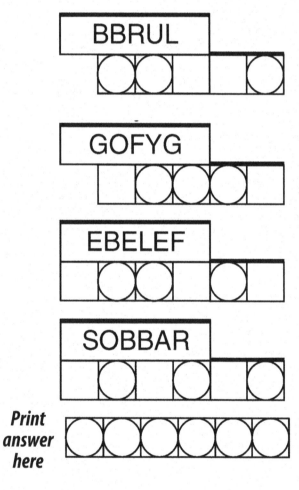

BBRUL

GOFYG

EBELEF

SOBBAR

Wow, Jenn! I don't think there are going to be leftovers.

Carve away!

Load me up!

WHEN THE DELECTABLE TURKEY WAS PUT ON THE TABLE, EVERYONE WAS ANXIOUS TO ----

Now arrange the circled letters to form the surprise answer, as suggested by the above cartoon.

Print answer here

JUMBLE®

Unscramble these four Jumbles, one letter
to each square, to form four ordinary words.

CRAFS

TINYU

CEOIXT

VERIEV

Let's start with the first of
these stockpiled boxcars.
Do I hear $1,000?

THE RAILROAD SOLD OFF
THEIR OLDER SURPLUS
BOXCARS BECAUSE THEY
WERE ---

Now arrange the circled letters
to form the surprise answer, as
suggested by the above cartoon.

Print
answer
here   " ◯◯ - ◯◯◯◯◯ - ◯◯◯◯ "

JUMBLE®

Unscramble these four Jumbles, one letter to each square, to form four ordinary words.

DORWL

NUSYN

TICATN

GILGEG

I'm glad we can continue to grow.

We'll be able to compete with the big nurseries soon.

Family Tree Nursery

40 Acres Available SOLD

WHEN THE PLANT NURSERY BOUGHT MORE LAND, THEY WERE THIS ON THEIR COMPETITION.

Now arrange the circled letters to form the surprise answer, as suggested by the above cartoon.

Print answer here

JUMBLE®

Unscramble these four Jumbles, one letter
to each square, to form four ordinary words.

CFOLK

UNVEE

SENLOS

GLIBRE

Should we
grab a bucket
of practice
balls?

Yes. We
should
warm up.

PLEASE HELP
YOURSELF.

THE TENNIS BALLS AT THE
COURTS WERE ---

Now arrange the circled letters
to form the surprise answer, as
suggested by the above cartoon.

**Print answer
here**

JUMBLE®

Unscramble these four Jumbles, one letter
to each square, to form four ordinary words.

LEEGA

POMOH

BLINEB

SPYMIK

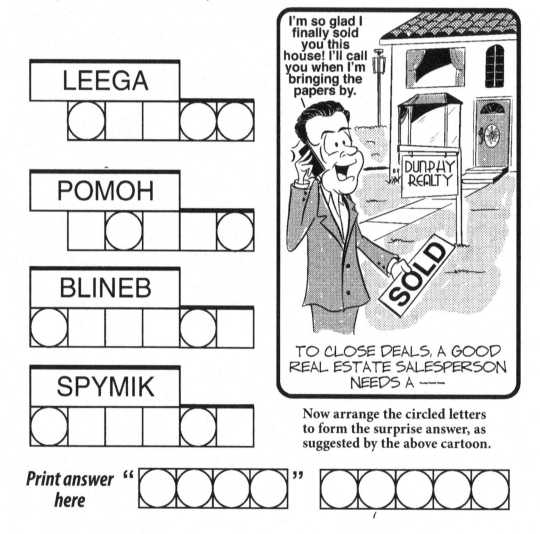

I'm so glad I finally sold you this house! I'll call you when I'm bringing the papers by.

DUNPHY REALTY

SOLD

TO CLOSE DEALS, A GOOD
REAL ESTATE SALESPERSON
NEEDS A ----

Now arrange the circled letters
to form the surprise answer, as
suggested by the above cartoon.

Print answer
here " ☐☐☐☐ " ☐☐☐☐☐

JUMBLE®

Unscramble these four Jumbles, one letter
to each square, to form four ordinary words.

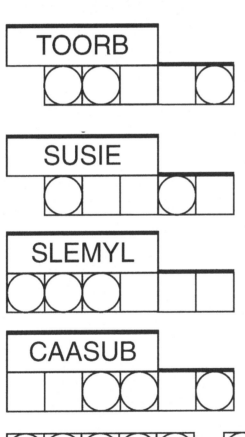

TOORB

SUSIE

SLEMYL

CAASUB

WHEN HIS SON SAID HE WAS
STARTING A ROCK BAND, IT
WASN'T ----

Now arrange the circled letters
to form the surprise answer, as
suggested by the above cartoon.

*Print
answer
here*

 HIS

JUMBLE®

Unscramble these four Jumbles, one letter
to each square, to form four ordinary words.

VEELL

BEATA

NOPYEL

DAZRIW

It's smaller than you need, but it's in your price range.

It's pretty run-down.

DUNPHY REALTY

THEY WANTED AN AFFORDABLE HOME, BUT THE ONE THEY LOOKED AT DIDN'T ———

Now arrange the circled letters
to form the surprise answer, as
suggested by the above cartoon.

Print answer here " ◯◯◯◯◯ " ◯◯◯◯

JUMBLE

Unscramble these four Jumbles, one letter
to each square, to form four ordinary words.

GISNE

SUDEO

DERGUT

TERLET

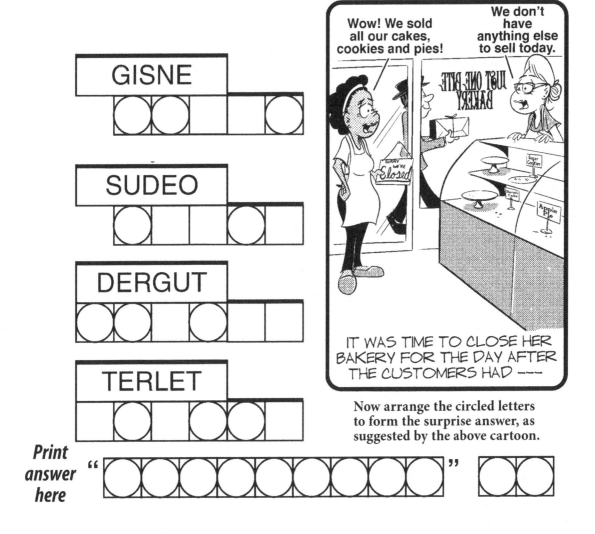

Wow! We sold
all our cakes,
cookies and pies!

We don't
have
anything else
to sell today.

JUST ONE BITE
BAKERY

IT WAS TIME TO CLOSE HER
BAKERY FOR THE DAY AFTER
THE CUSTOMERS HAD ---

Now arrange the circled letters
to form the surprise answer, as
suggested by the above cartoon.

Print answer here " ☐☐☐☐☐☐☐☐☐ " ☐☐

JUMBLE®

Unscramble these four Jumbles, one letter to each square, to form four ordinary words.

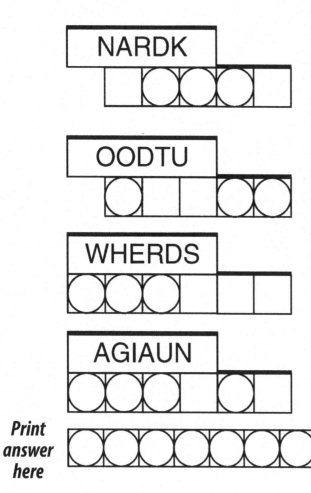

NARDK

OODTU

WHERDS

AGIAUN

Behave, or I'm going to stop this ride!

You know better!

Cam, stop that!

THE KIDS ON THE CARNIVAL'S CAROUSEL WERE ----

Now arrange the circled letters to form the surprise answer, as suggested by the above cartoon.

Print answer here

JUMBLE®

Unscramble these four Jumbles, one letter
to each square, to form four ordinary words.

FINSF

TINNH

FLEKIC

ALGGGE

Dude, you're going to lose.

I think you're right.

And finally, eight ball in the corner.

AFTER WATCHING HIS
OPPONENT MAKE SHOT AFTER
SHOT, HE WAS GETTING A ----

Now arrange the circled letters
to form the surprise answer, as
suggested by the above cartoon.

**Print
answer
here**

93

JUMBLE®

Unscramble these four Jumbles, one letter
to each square, to form four ordinary words.

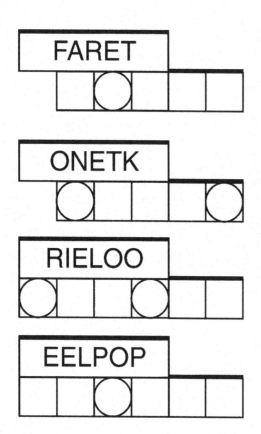

FARET

ONETK

RIELOO

EELPOP

Sydney's Shoes

Grand Opening

We're here.

I'm excited about this new store. It was worth the 15-minute walk.

CUSTOMERS ARRIVED AT THE
NEW SHOE STORE ----

Now arrange the circled letters
to form the surprise answer, as
suggested by the above cartoon.

Print answer here ☐☐ ☐☐☐☐

JUMBLE®

Unscramble these four Jumbles, one letter
to each square, to form four ordinary words.

HENTT

DOYLD

SLWARP

CEPIEA

I can't believe you're retiring.

Yes, a few more deposits to my 401k, and I see sunny days ahead.

PALM READING

$100

THE PALM READER SAVED A
LOT OF MONEY, AND NOW
RETIREMENT WAS ----

Now arrange the circled letters
to form the surprise answer, as
suggested by the above cartoon.

Print
answer
here

JUMBLE ®

Unscramble these four Jumbles, one letter
to each square, to form four ordinary words.

VUMEA

GIRBN

RILTEP

MAMHYE

I think I'll
use this
one!

These are
all great!
Hey, look–
a rainbow!

THE LEPRECHAUN WHO GREW
HIS OWN SHAMROCKS
HAD A ---

Now arrange the circled letters
to form the surprise answer, as
suggested by the above cartoon.

Print
answer
here

JUMBLE®

Unscramble these four Jumbles, one letter to each square, to form four ordinary words.

CATLH

RILEN

SOMTAC

LAGEEL

AI, what are you doing?

I made an error. I need to start over.

HE ERASED THE FORMULA FROM THE CHALKBOARD TO START OVER WITH A ---

Now arrange the circled letters to form the surprise answer, as suggested by the above cartoon.

Print answer here

JUMBLE®

Unscramble these four Jumbles, one letter
to each square, to form four ordinary words.

CERPH

AHCOV

FDOBIR

CURPES

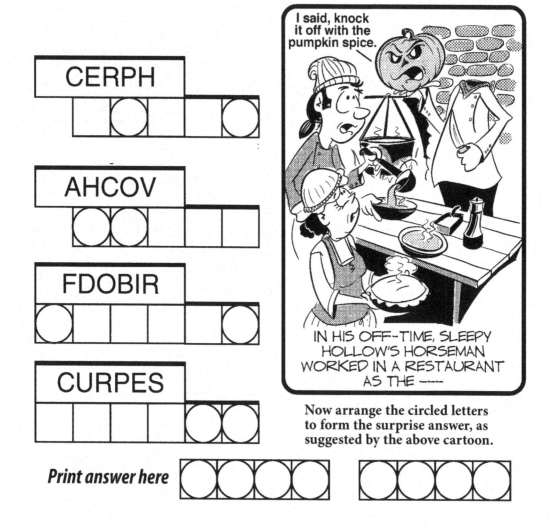

I said, knock
it off with the
pumpkin spice.

IN HIS OFF-TIME, SLEEPY
HOLLOW'S HORSEMAN
WORKED IN A RESTAURANT
AS THE ----

Now arrange the circled letters
to form the surprise answer, as
suggested by the above cartoon.

Print answer here

JUMBLE®

Unscramble these four Jumbles, one letter to each square, to form four ordinary words.

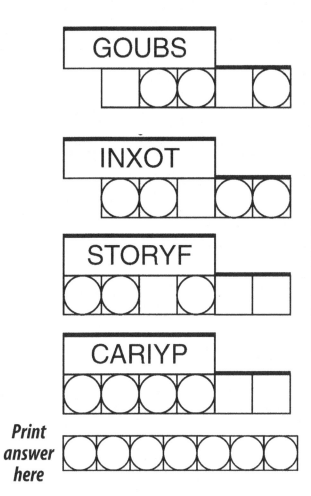

GOUBS

INXOT

STORYF

CARIYP

You can see our continued success.

Stocks are up.

Now we can get started on the 747.

WITH THE SUCCESS OF THE 707, THE BOEING COMPANY HAD ---

Now arrange the circled letters to form the surprise answer, as suggested by the above cartoon.

Print answer here

JUMBLE®

Unscramble these four Jumbles, one letter to each square, to form four ordinary words.

GUBYG

KALEY

CINTEE

TRUUEF

I don't think that's a good sound.

Was that your stomach? I told you that mayo was old.

GLURRBB

HE WASN'T POSITIVE HE HAD FOOD POISONING, BUT HE HAD A ———

Now arrange the circled letters to form the surprise answer, as suggested by the above cartoon.

Print answer here

JUMBLE®

Unscramble these four Jumbles, one letter
to each square, to form four ordinary words.

VODIT

ESYDE

XLYGAA

LMMEEB

GOOD KNIGHT CLUB

I turned 40 today. Join me for an ale?

Wow! I'm 40, too! We're getting up there.

THE 40-YEAR-OLD KNIGHTS
IN THE 1300S HAD ----

Now arrange the circled letters
to form the surprise answer, as
suggested by the above cartoon.

Print
answer
here

◯◯◯◯◯◯ - ◯◯◯◯

JUMBLE®

Unscramble these four Jumbles, one letter
to each square, to form four ordinary words.

POLEE

RITEG

TRAGEH

UNNLAA

I can hunt from
far away with this.
Plus, it's light to
carry. I can also
fish with it!

Club, good!
Stick, not!

THEY DISAGREED ABOUT
WHICH WEAPON WAS BEST
AND CONTINUED TO ---

Now arrange the circled letters
to form the surprise answer, as
suggested by the above cartoon.

Print
answer
here

JUMBLE ®

Unscramble these four Jumbles, one letter
to each square, to form four ordinary words.

XBREO

PYMET

CLAPAA

COSTEK

WE CAN NEVER TRULY
COMPENSATE THOSE WHO
FOUGHT FOR OUR COUNTRY,
BUT WE CAN ----

Now arrange the circled letters
to form the surprise answer, as
suggested by the above cartoon.

*Print
answer
here*

JUMBLE®

Unscramble these four Jumbles, one letter
to each square, to form four ordinary words.

What's in the paper?

It's all about Hillary and Norgay reaching the peak of Everest.

London Herald

EVEREST CONQUERED!

British Expediti
Reaches Summi
Coronation Da

The Highest Challenge

TYRPA

SOPIE

PLIRPE

TCLEKO

WHEN EDMUND HILLARY AND
TENZING NORGAY REACHED
EVEREST'S PEAK, IT WAS A ----

Now arrange the circled letters
to form the surprise answer, as
suggested by the above cartoon.

Print answer here

JUMBLE®

Unscramble these four Jumbles, one letter
to each square, to form four ordinary words.

KSADE

UHISS

CODEKT

THACYT

We help all our
customers with
their lock needs.

Can you
duplicate
this?

Of course
we can!

THE LOCKSMITH HAD GREAT
CUSTOMER SERVICE, WHICH HE
CONSIDERED TO BE A ----

Now arrange the circled letters
to form the surprise answer, as
suggested by the above cartoon.

*Print
answer
here*

105

JUMBLE®

Unscramble these four Jumbles, one letter to each square, to form four ordinary words.

PINYP

GLAEE

SOLTEC

TLAHEH

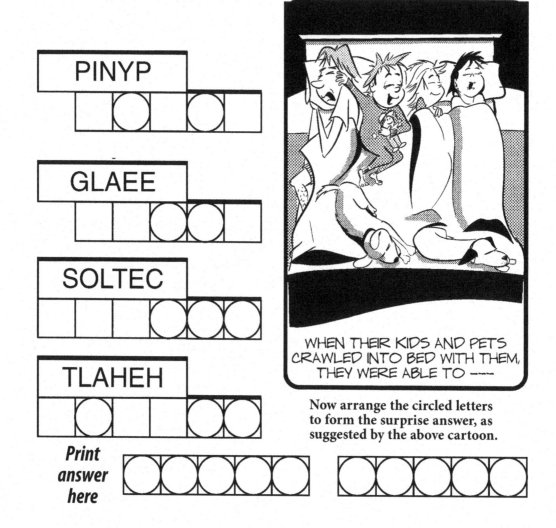

WHEN THEIR KIDS AND PETS CRAWLED INTO BED WITH THEM, THEY WERE ABLE TO ----

Now arrange the circled letters to form the surprise answer, as suggested by the above cartoon.

Print answer here

JUMBLE ®

Unscramble these four Jumbles, one letter
to each square, to form four ordinary words.

GRUPE

VEYHA

CIPTEO

MENDTA

JUMBLE MOTORS

Since we added a Jumble solver feature, the demand has risen and so has the price.

I'll take it.

What is, "OCAMIS" unjumbled?

MOSAIC

THE POPULAR CAR MODEL'S PRICE WAS BEING ---

Now arrange the circled letters
to form the surprise answer, as
suggested by the above cartoon.

Print answer here ⬡⬡⬡⬡⬡⬡ ⬡⬡

JUMBLE

Unscramble these four Jumbles, one letter to each square, to form four ordinary words.

ANGIT
◯◯◯◯☐

DUSKO
☐◯◯◯◯

ANHECC
◯☐◯◯☐☐

LOVETR
◯☐☐◯◯◯

Class of 2017

We made up a new "word" for you girls.

What is it, Mr. Knurek?

Is it "punny," Dad?

WHEN THEY FINISHED HIGH SCHOOL, HE COMPLIMENTED THEM ALL BY SAYING ---

Now arrange the circled letters to form the surprise answer, as suggested by the above cartoon.

Print answer here " ◯◯◯◯◯◯◯◯◯◯◯◯◯◯◯◯◯ "

JUMBLE®

Unscramble these four Jumbles, one letter
to each square, to form four ordinary words.

HHCAT

KVOEE

DUGRON

SPYRAT

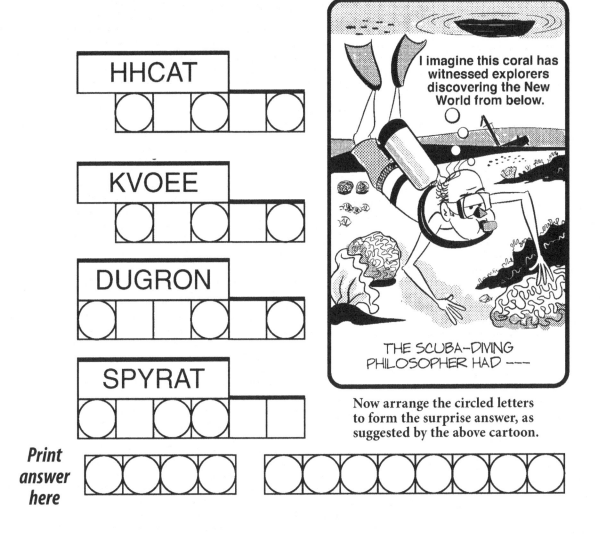

I imagine this coral has
witnessed explorers
discovering the New
World from below.

THE SCUBA-DIVING
PHILOSOPHER HAD ---

Now arrange the circled letters
to form the surprise answer, as
suggested by the above cartoon.

*Print
answer
here*

109

JUMBLE®

Unscramble these four Jumbles, one letter
to each square, to form four ordinary words.

GUEJD

BATHI

LNBUED

LORALD

Good news,
gentlemen. You've
been chosen to take
her off the ground.

We won't let
you down.

THEY WOULD PILOT THE FIRST
BOEING 747 TEST FLIGHT NOW
THAT THEY'D ----

Now arrange the circled letters
to form the surprise answer, as
suggested by the above cartoon.

*Print
answer
here*

JUMBLE®

Unscramble these four Jumbles, one letter to each square, to form four ordinary words.

RUKNT

UTOBA

SKYCOT

CRAFTO

I think I need new shoes.

Are you kidding? We're getting you back in shape. Let's start with a long run.

THE SPRINTER WAS LOSING RACES AND NEEDED TO TRAIN HARDER TO GET HIS CAREER ---

Now arrange the circled letters to form the surprise answer, as suggested by the above cartoon.

Print answer here

JUMBLE®

Unscramble these four Jumbles, one letter to each square, to form four ordinary words.

INNOO

SHOTI

OWALTU

WADDEN

I told you that I want the receptionist desk moved by my lab.

We've been trying as hard as we can to make it all fit.

WHEN THE DENTIST AND THE CARPENTER ARGUED ABOUT THE CONSTRUCTION, THEY FOUGHT ----

Now arrange the circled letters to form the surprise answer, as suggested by the above cartoon.

Print answer here

JUMBLE®

Unscramble these four Jumbles, one letter to each square, to form four ordinary words.

SALTN

OSUHE

IBLAVE

FINNAT

... and finally, almonds. That's it!

Wow! How do you know so much?

THE SQUIRREL WAS ABLE TO SUMMARIZE HIS LOVE OF PECANS, CASHEWS AND ALMONDS ---

Now arrange the circled letters to form the surprise answer, as suggested by the above cartoon.

Print answer here

JUMBLE®

Unscramble these four Jumbles, one letter
to each square, to form four ordinary words.

TEONF

AILSA

PWENEH

ASIROL

Where am I supposed to sit?

You're the one who lets them on the furniture.

THE TIRED DOGS TURNED
THE COUCH INTO A ---

Now arrange the circled letters
to form the surprise answer, as
suggested by the above cartoon.

Print
answer
here

JUMBLE ®

Unscramble these four Jumbles, one letter to each square, to form four ordinary words.

IMCMI

VAUAG

WADNET

TIRAGU

What do you say, Jake?
Are you ready to go to
Montrose Beach to
play ball?

WHEN IS A DOG'S
TAIL NOT A TAIL?
WHEN IT'S A ---

Now arrange the circled letters to form the surprise answer, as suggested by the above cartoon.

Print answer here " ⬡⬡⬡⬡⬡⬡ " "

JUMBLE®

Unscramble these four Jumbles, one letter
to each square, to form four ordinary words.

TREPU

MASHE

ORIHAD

FIRDAT

My plan is to travel
along the banks of
the Hudson River.

According to
my maps,
that's the
best way.

"SLEEPY HOLLOW
MIDDLE SCHOOL"

SLEEPY HOLLOW'S HORSEMAN
NEEDED TO GET TO
NEW YORK CITY, SO HE ----

Now arrange the circled letters
to form the surprise answer, as
suggested by the above cartoon.

**Print
answer
here**

JUMBLE®

Unscramble these four Jumbles, one letter to each square, to form four ordinary words.

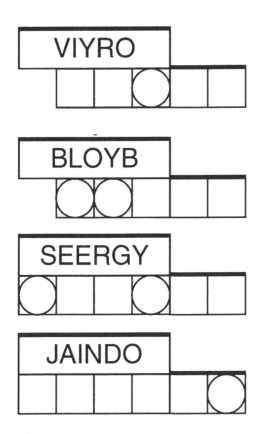

VIYRO

BLOYB

SEERGY

JAINDO

FOR THEM, SAYING GOODBYE TOOK ———

Now arrange the circled letters to form the surprise answer, as suggested by the above cartoon.

Print answer here

117

JUMBLE®

Unscramble these four Jumbles, one letter
to each square, to form four ordinary words.

GECYA

DOORE

NIDIEV

CURPEK

I guess it's ladies first.

You've got that right.

THE ROOSTER WOULD HAVE TO WAIT TO EAT BECAUSE THERE WAS A ----

Now arrange the circled letters
to form the surprise answer, as
suggested by the above cartoon.

*Print
answer
here*

JUMBLE®

Unscramble these four Jumbles, one letter
to each square, to form four ordinary words.

NPOYH

LEHOL

DIFELD

GIXTAN

AFTER LANDING IN HAWAII,
THEY GOT THE ---

Now arrange the circled letters
to form the surprise answer, as
suggested by the above cartoon.

*Print
answer
here*

"⬡⬡⬡" ⬡⬡ ⬡⬡⬡ ⬡⬡⬡⬡

JUMBLE®

Unscramble these four Jumbles, one letter to each square, to form four ordinary words.

CWMAA

CRASF

BRAROH

TIEUYQ

I can't believe you made all of this today!

I'm so glad I'm going into fashion design. I just can't stop.

SHE LOVED MAKING DRESSES BY HAND ---

Now arrange the circled letters to form the surprise answer, as suggested by the above cartoon.

Print answer here " ⬡⬡⬡ " ⬡⬡⬡⬡

JUMBLE®

Unscramble these four Jumbles, one letter
to each square, to form four ordinary words.

GILCO

NOCAG

DYNEOK

RUJINO

Now arrange the circled letters
to form the surprise answer, as
suggested by the above cartoon.

Print
answer
here

121

JUMBLE®

Unscramble these four Jumbles, one letter
to each square, to form four ordinary words.

ORNCO

IPTOL

BREHOT

CABFIR

I'm so glad I finally matched him.

Way to hustle, Pete!

BEFORE PETE ROSE TOOK OVER AS THE ALL-TIME HIT LEADER, HE HAD TO ---

Now arrange the circled letters
to form the surprise answer, as
suggested by the above cartoon.

Print answer here "◯◯◯" ◯◯◯◯

JUMBLE®

Unscramble these four Jumbles, one letter
to each square, to form four ordinary words.

YUJIC

NEPDU

BEBOWL

TAGRYE

You lads look great!

Yeah, yeah, yeah.

He knows what he's doing.

THE BARBER WHO CUT
THE BEATLES' HAIR IN
1963 DID A ---

Now arrange the circled letters
to form the surprise answer, as
suggested by the above cartoon.

*Print
answer
here*

◯◯◯◯ - ◯◯ ◯◯◯

JUMBLE®

Unscramble these four Jumbles, one letter to each square, to form four ordinary words.

NETGA

HNUCB

UNORNE

CTIEWK

Look at these kids. They're like zombies.

Put those things down and go into the woods.

THE SPIDERS THOUGHT THEIR KIDS WERE SPENDING TOO MUCH TIME ----

Now arrange the circled letters to form the surprise answer, as suggested by the above cartoon.

Print answer here

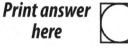

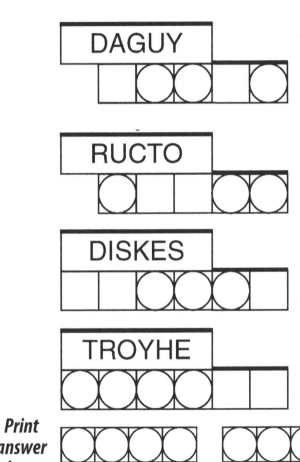

JUMBLE®

Unscramble these four Jumbles, one letter
to each square, to form four ordinary words.

DAGUY

RUCTO

DISKES

TROYHE

I just don't think I'll ever get better.

Just be patient and keep doing what you're doing. You'll get there.

THE STRUGGLING YOUNG
GOLFER WANTED TO QUIT,
BUT HER COACH
RECOMMENDED SHE ----

Now arrange the circled letters
to form the surprise answer, as
suggested by the above cartoon.

Print answer here

JUMBLE®

Unscramble these four Jumbles, one letter to each square, to form four ordinary words.

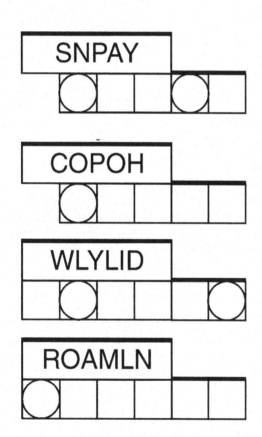

SNPAY

COPOH

WLYLID

ROAMLN

Can I borrow those for a second?

You better cut out the attitude, young lady.

Do I look like I'm done using them? Find your own pair.

SHE WANTED TO BORROW THE SCISSORS, BUT HER SISTER WAS BEING ----

Now arrange the circled letters to form the surprise answer, as suggested by the above cartoon.

Print answer here

126

JUMBLE®

Unscramble these four Jumbles, one letter to each square, to form four ordinary words.

CINME

UKAQC

KOIREO

ARUBUE

THE BABY DELIVERED AT 30,000 FEET WAS ----

Now arrange the circled letters to form the surprise answer, as suggested by the above cartoon.

Print answer here

JUMBLE®

Unscramble these four Jumbles, one letter
to each square, to form four ordinary words.

CAKNK

DAGRU

SATUCC

MEGILN

Could you keep it down?

THE TENNIS PLAYER COULDN'T
FIND HIS EQUIPMENT IN THE
CLOSET AND WAS ----

Now arrange the circled letters
to form the surprise answer, as
suggested by the above cartoon.

*Print
answer
here*

128

JUMBLE®

Unscramble these four Jumbles, one letter
to each square, to form four ordinary words.

TUYPT

SUDEO

GOCCAN

BNILEM

This is the
"Seinfeld" when
Kramer creates
the "Bro".

That's
funny.
I just love
the feel of
our new
couch.

WHEN THE COUPLE TRIED OUT
THEIR NEW FURNITURE WHILE
WATCHING TV, THEY
WATCHED A ----

Now arrange the circled letters
to form the surprise answer, as
suggested by the above cartoon.

Print answer here

JUMBLE®

Unscramble these four Jumbles, one letter
to each square, to form four ordinary words.

VROGE

COLTU

OLODED

PRICST

I should've
made a
reservation.

I didn't think
they'd be
busy tonight.

HE TOLD HIS WIFE THERE
WOULDN'T BE A LONG LINE,
BUT HE ----

Now arrange the circled letters
to form the surprise answer, as
suggested by the above cartoon.

*Print
answer
here*

130

JUMBLE®

Unscramble these four Jumbles, one letter
to each square, to form four ordinary words.

WYLOL

PODTA

RHOFUT

GULAPE

How high
would you
like to go?

Whoa! This is
so much
better than
stairs!

Is it
safe?

WHEN ELEVATORS IN BUILDINGS
STARTED TO BECOME
POPULAR, PEOPLE WERE ---

Now arrange the circled letters
to form the surprise answer, as
suggested by the above cartoon.

Print answer here

JUMBLE®

Unscramble these four Jumbles, one letter
to each square, to form four ordinary words.

GNEUL

SLEWH

TACINP

ROLFAM

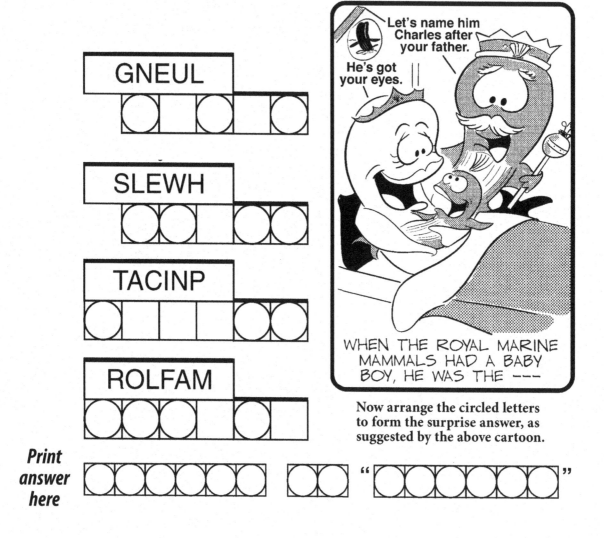

Let's name him
Charles after
your father.

He's got
your eyes.

WHEN THE ROYAL MARINE
MAMMALS HAD A BABY
BOY, HE WAS THE ---

Now arrange the circled letters
to form the surprise answer, as
suggested by the above cartoon.

Print
answer
here

[ ][ ][ ][ ][ ][ ][ ]   [ ][ ]   " [ ][ ][ ][ ][ ][ ][ ] "

JUMBLE®

Unscramble these four Jumbles, one letter
to each square, to form four ordinary words.

IGAME

GYROL

YEHHNP

RWASLP

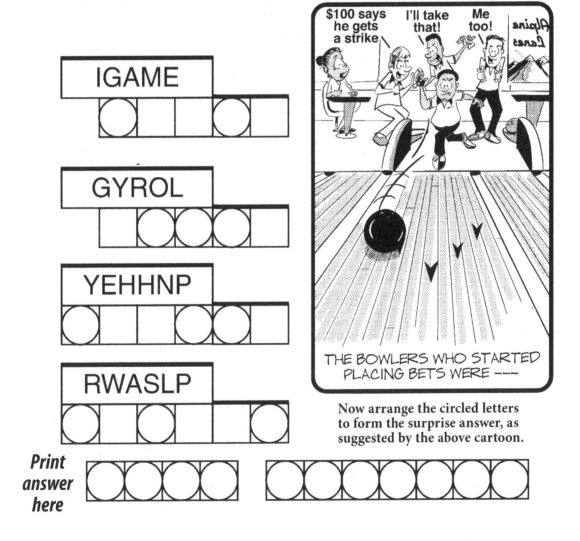

$100 says
he gets
a strike

I'll take
that!

Me
too!

Alpine
Lanes

THE BOWLERS WHO STARTED
PLACING BETS WERE ---

Now arrange the circled letters
to form the surprise answer, as
suggested by the above cartoon.

Print
answer
here

133

JUMBLE®

Unscramble these four Jumbles, one letter
to each square, to form four ordinary words.

CUPHO

ONRIY

LIPRAL

GLIYHH

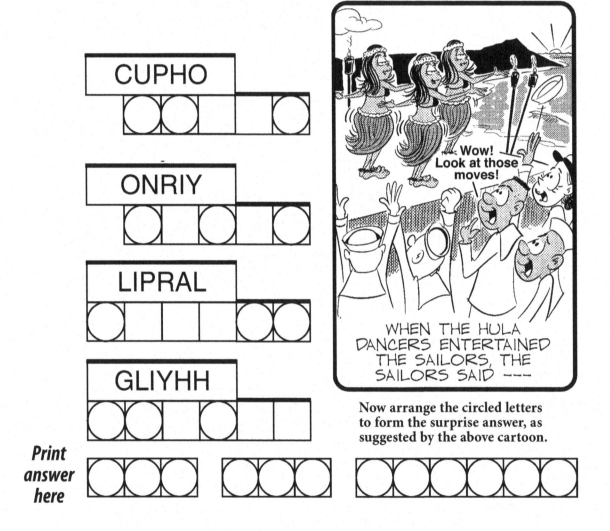

Wow!
Look at those
moves!

WHEN THE HULA
DANCERS ENTERTAINED
THE SAILORS, THE
SAILORS SAID ---

Now arrange the circled letters
to form the surprise answer, as
suggested by the above cartoon.

*Print
answer
here*

JUMBLE®

Unscramble these four Jumbles, one letter to each square, to form four ordinary words.

SOCRS

LECRI

VRUDEO

SUPMCA

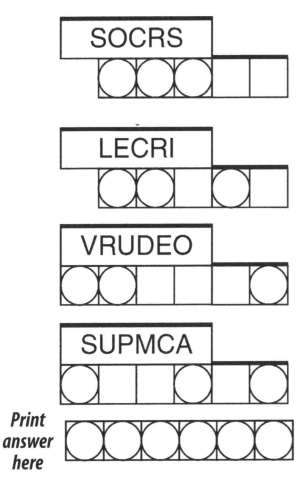

Why does this cost $1,000 more than it did last week?

They just auctioned one for that much.

No Refunds!

THE CLASSIC VINYL ALBUMS WERE SELLING FOR ---

Now arrange the circled letters to form the surprise answer, as suggested by the above cartoon.

Print answer here

135

JUMBLE®

Unscramble these four Jumbles, one letter
to each square, to form four ordinary words.

DOFOL

CULYK

WYOLSL

TNIKET

TO GET MORE CUSTOMERS,
THE LOCKSMITH SET UP A ----

Now arrange the circled letters
to form the surprise answer, as
suggested by the above cartoon.

Print answer here " ◯◯◯ - ◯◯◯◯ "

JUMBLE®

Unscramble these four Jumbles, one letter to each square, to form four ordinary words.

BEATA

LORTL

PHSSLA

TETAST

WHEN THEY BUILT THE NEW ROUNDABOUT, THEY PULLED OUT ----

Now arrange the circled letters to form the surprise answer, as suggested by the above cartoon.

Print answer here

JUMBLE®

Unscramble these four Jumbles, one letter
to each square, to form four ordinary words.

HURES

LEYID

GUNLEP

DSOETD

How can he nap
through all this
noise?

I guess
he's tired.

HE DOZED OFF LISTENING TO
MUSIC ON HIS HEADPHONES,
AND WAS ABLE TO ———

Now arrange the circled letters
to form the surprise answer, as
suggested by the above cartoon.

*Print
answer
here*

JUMBLE®

Unscramble these four Jumbles, one letter to each square, to form four ordinary words.

GORRI

PRAGH

WUTOIT

TAUDEP

We need to expand. We need more bamboo for the new hut resort.

This island is really booming.

MINNOW NURSERY

THE NURSERY THAT SOLD BAMBOO WAS EXPERIENCING ---

Now arrange the circled letters to form the surprise answer, as suggested by the above cartoon.

Print answer here

139

JUMBLE®

Unscramble these four Jumbles, one letter to each square, to form four ordinary words.

PRUUS

RUDOG

NARMEN

WUNIES

SHE WANTED HER DAUGHTER TO CLEAN HER ROOM AND WASN'T ---

Now arrange the circled letters to form the surprise answer, as suggested by the above cartoon.

Print answer here

140

JUMBLE®

Unscramble these four Jumbles, one letter
to each square, to form four ordinary words.

KOLAP

LUDFI

GENAMA

TGUINO

Get a
close-up
of her toes
wiggling.

GRAND
OPENING!

Will this be
on tonight's
news?

Got
it.

TO COVER THE OPENING OF
THE NEW SHOE STORE, THE TV
NEWS CREW NEEDED ---

Now arrange the circled letters
to form the surprise answer, as
suggested by the above cartoon.

Print answer here

JUMBLE®

Unscramble these four Jumbles, one letter
to each square, to form four ordinary words.

FALCO

BOTRO

WOLLFO

CALTEK

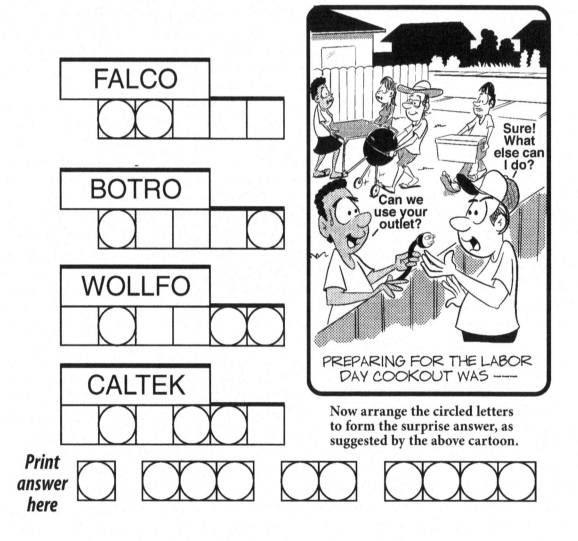

Sure!
What
else can
I do?

Can we
use your
outlet?

PREPARING FOR THE LABOR
DAY COOKOUT WAS ----

Now arrange the circled letters
to form the surprise answer, as
suggested by the above cartoon.

*Print
answer
here*

142

JUMBLE®

Unscramble these four Jumbles, one letter
to each square, to form four ordinary words.

OMESO

NITUP

BNLIEB

RLAMYW

It rides really rough.
But I think you're
onto something.

I'm going
to keep
chiseling
away at it.

THE WHEEL HADN'T QUITE
BEEN INVENTED, BUT THE
WHEELS ‒‒‒

Now arrange the circled letters
to form the surprise answer, as
suggested by the above cartoon.

*Print
answer
here*

JUMBLE®

Unscramble these four Jumbles, one letter
to each square, to form four ordinary words.

GATRN

NHORO

TISNIS

DORNET

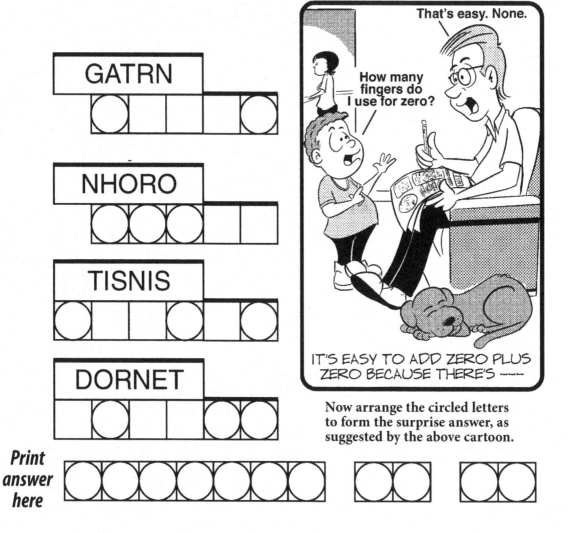

That's easy. None.

How many fingers do I use for zero?

IT'S EASY TO ADD ZERO PLUS
ZERO BECAUSE THERE'S ----

Now arrange the circled letters
to form the surprise answer, as
suggested by the above cartoon.

*Print
answer
here*

JUMBLE®

Unscramble these four Jumbles, one letter
to each square, to form four ordinary words.

TLAWZ

CETLE

NIHISF

EENVLE

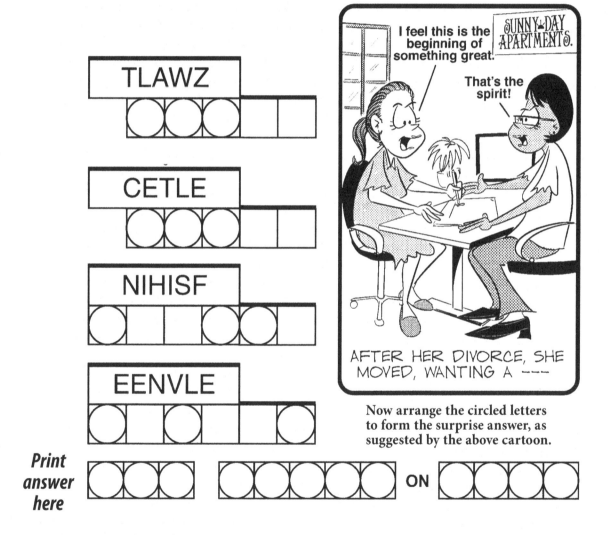

I feel this is the beginning of something great!

SUNNY-DAY APARTMENTS.

That's the spirit!

AFTER HER DIVORCE, SHE MOVED, WANTING A ---

Now arrange the circled letters
to form the surprise answer, as
suggested by the above cartoon.

Print answer here

ON

JUMBLE®

Unscramble these four Jumbles, one letter
to each square, to form four ordinary words.

TCOBH

CEWIN

TABYNO

KEWYEL

We're on a roll.   Yep. Let's see what they do tomorrow.

THE BASEBALL TEAM'S WINNING STREAK CONTINUED ---

Now arrange the circled letters
to form the surprise answer, as
suggested by the above cartoon.

Print
answer
here   " ◯◯◯ " ◯◯ " ◯◯◯ "

146

JUMBLE®

Unscramble these four Jumbles, one letter
to each square, to form four ordinary words.

DUYDM

SORAE

KRIHNS

PRUBAL

My 2.5 million Photogram
followers must think
I need more money.

You're right! You'll
be making a pretty
penny.

MALE MODELS WITH
SUCCESSFUL CAREERS ARE ----

Now arrange the circled letters
to form the surprise answer, as
suggested by the above cartoon.

*Print
answer
here*

JUMBLE®

Unscramble these four Jumbles, one letter
to each square, to form four ordinary words.

ZORRA

TIHAF

COREKT

ROMMEY

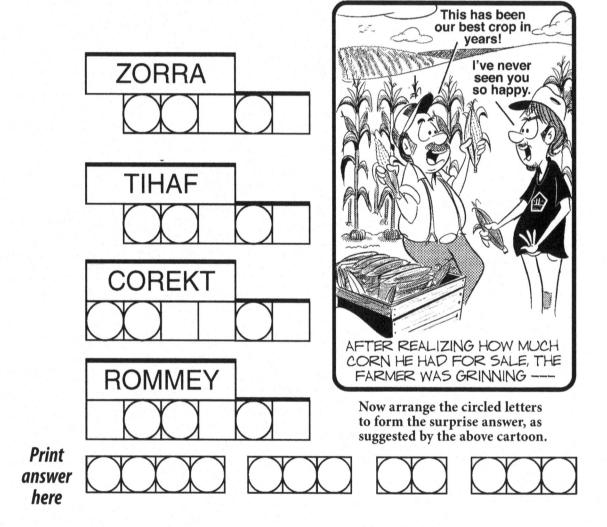

This has been
our best crop in
years!

I've never
seen you
so happy.

AFTER REALIZING HOW MUCH
CORN HE HAD FOR SALE, THE
FARMER WAS GRINNING ———

Now arrange the circled letters
to form the surprise answer, as
suggested by the above cartoon.

*Print
answer
here*

JUMBLE®

Unscramble these four Jumbles, one letter
to each square, to form four ordinary words.

SFRAC

PULIP

TLEGNY

CLORSL

THE LAUNDROMAT THAT
INSTALLED EXERCISE
EQUIPMENT FEATURED ---

Now arrange the circled letters
to form the surprise answer, as
suggested by the above cartoon.

Print answer here

JUMBLE®

Unscramble these four Jumbles, one letter
to each square, to form four ordinary words.

DUBIL

MOICC

LFENAL

DURISA

How did we forget a
seventh puzzle?

Quick! Help me! I dropped my stylus in the trash, and I can't find it!

WHEN THE JUMBLE CREATORS
REALIZED THEY'D FORGOTTEN
TO MAKE A PUZZLE, THEY ----

Now arrange the circled letters
to form the surprise answer, as
suggested by the above cartoon.

Print answer here

JUMBLE®

Unscramble these four Jumbles, one letter to each square, to form four ordinary words.

XROPY

JANOB

PESDEY

CDIWEK

I am never swimming in the ocean again.

WHEN AUDIENCES WATCHED THIS 1975 FILM ABOUT A GREAT WHITE SHARK, THEIR ---

Now arrange the circled letters to form the surprise answer, as suggested by the above cartoon.

Print answer here

151

JUMBLE®

Unscramble these four Jumbles, one letter
to each square, to form four ordinary words.

TOUSC

DOPAT

GNERED

LUYELP

Half off
your
listing?

You're
being too
generous.

My husband is a
veteran and it's an
honor to help out the
two, soon to be three,
of you.

THE LANDLORD
REDUCED THE YOUNG
COUPLE'S RENT, SAYING
IT WAS THE ---

Now arrange the circled letters
to form the surprise answer, as
suggested by the above cartoon.

Print
answer
here

" ◯◯◯◯◯◯ " SHE ◯◯◯◯◯◯ ◯◯

JUMBLE ®

Unscramble these four Jumbles, one letter
to each square, to form four ordinary words.

SINOB

TEMLA

MBEFLU

VORPNE

Now, I have a special way of explaining this that I've been using for ten years.

MULTIPLICATION

THE MATH TEACHER
HAD TAUGHT
MULTIPLICATION A ---

Now arrange the circled letters
to form the surprise answer, as
suggested by the above cartoon.

*Print
answer
here*

JUMBLE®

Unscramble these four Jumbles, one letter
to each square, to form four ordinary words.

ROSYR

BREYR

TIEPOC

BETEAD

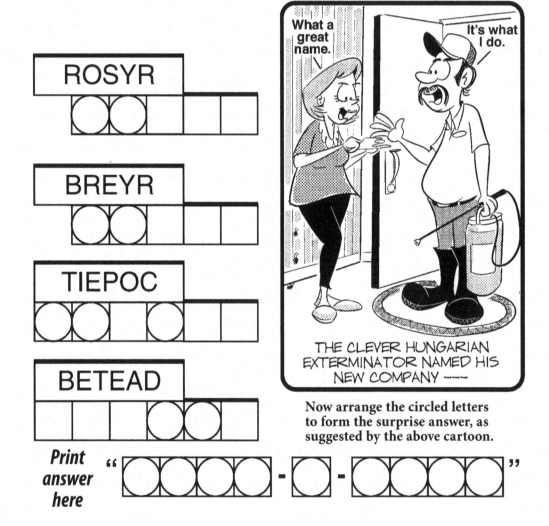

What a
great
name.

It's what
I do.

THE CLEVER HUNGARIAN
EXTERMINATOR NAMED HIS
NEW COMPANY ----

Now arrange the circled letters
to form the surprise answer, as
suggested by the above cartoon.

*Print
answer
here* " ◯◯◯◯ - ◯ - ◯◯◯◯ "

JUMBLE®

Unscramble these four Jumbles, one letter
to each square, to form four ordinary words.

VECOT

EPMTT

FITSHY

RIMFON

THE NEW DISCOUNT
RETAILER'S CUSTOMERS
HAD GREAT DEALS ---

Now arrange the circled letters
to form the surprise answer, as
suggested by the above cartoon.

Print
answer
here

☐☐ ☐☐☐☐☐ FOR ☐☐☐☐

155

JUMBLE®

Unscramble these four Jumbles, one letter to each square, to form four ordinary words.

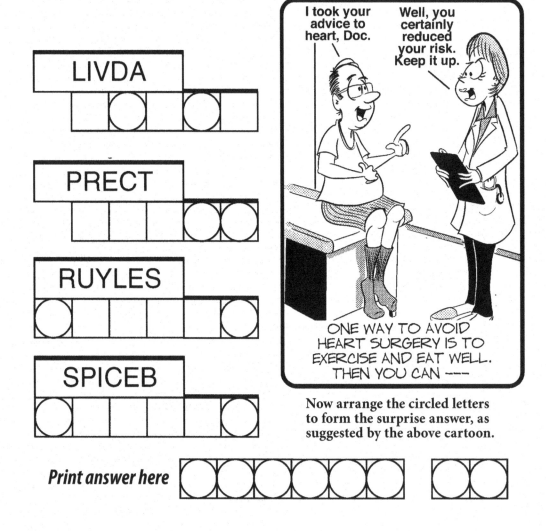

LIVDA

PRECT

RUYLES

SPICEB

I took your advice to heart, Doc.

Well, you certainly reduced your risk. Keep it up.

ONE WAY TO AVOID HEART SURGERY IS TO EXERCISE AND EAT WELL. THEN YOU CAN ----

Now arrange the circled letters to form the surprise answer, as suggested by the above cartoon.

Print answer here

JUMBLE®

Unscramble these four Jumbles, one letter
to each square, to form four ordinary words.

NIHYS

VEGAL

TRIBET

GRETER

Which way are we headed?

I think we're close to St. Lawrence Island.

RUSSIA   ALASKA

We're headed west.

THE ALASKAN FISHING-BOAT
CAPTAIN WAS DISORIENTED
AND NEEDED TO GET HIS---

Now arrange the circled letters
to form the surprise answer, as
suggested by the above cartoon.

*Print
answer
here*   " _ _ _ _ _ _   _ _ _ _ _ _ "

JUMBLE®

Unscramble these four Jumbles, one letter to each square, to form four ordinary words.

GGION

DYOLD

FEDDIE

CCESIN

Before I begin, I'd like to get some info from you. I want to make sure we get just the right style.

I appreciate you being so thorough.

TO GET INFORMATION BEFORE CUTTING HAIR, THE SALON OWNER DID ----

Now arrange the circled letters to form the surprise answer, as suggested by the above cartoon.

Print answer here " ⬡⬡ " ⬡⬡⬡⬡⬡⬡⬡⬡⬡

JUMBLE®

Unscramble these four Jumbles, one letter
to each square, to form four ordinary words.

NODMU

SAYET

LWWIOL

STAGEK

With the rave reviews of our latest line, I feel now is the time to walk away.

She's my fashion hero.

She's so classy.

THE FASHION DESIGNER RETIRED AT THE TOP OF HER CAREER SO THAT SHE COULD ---

Now arrange the circled letters
to form the surprise answer, as
suggested by the above cartoon.

*Print
answer
here*

JUMBLE®

Unscramble these four Jumbles, one letter to each square, to form four ordinary words.

CUHHT

MEECE

RAYALS

TYUJLS

Morning! Ready for breakfast?

WHEN THE FARMER GREETED THE HORSES AT FEEDING TIME, HE SAID ----

Now arrange the circled letters to form the surprise answer, as suggested by the above cartoon.

Print answer here " ◯◯◯ " ◯◯◯◯◯

JUMBLE®

Unscramble these four Jumbles, one letter to each square, to form four ordinary words.

LOAKA

LRIGL

FIMDEF

TERNEL

But we had a reservation!

It's all right, big guy.

I don't have enough food or room for you.

KONG HAD TROUBLE FINDING A MEAL THAT WAS ----

Now arrange the circled letters to form the surprise answer, as suggested by the above cartoon.

Print answer here

JUMBLE.

Unscramble these four Jumbles, one letter
to each square, to form four ordinary words.

OUNNI

SIVAT

EREPEK

RACGLI

Now, you need to
extend your paw
and tail to show
where it's at.

TO HELP THE YOUNG HUNTING
DOG LEARN, THE EXPERIENCED
HUNTING DOG ----

Now arrange the circled letters
to form the surprise answer, as
suggested by the above cartoon.

Print
answer
here

JUMBLE®

Unscramble these six Jumbles, one letter to each square, to form six ordinary words.

PERUSH

GLEGGI

CINUDE

BARTUN

CLOMPY

YONKED

WHY THE HORSE
GALLOPED
OVER THE HILL.

CLOSED

Now arrange the circled letters to form the surprise answer, as suggested by the above cartoon.

Print answer here

HE ⃝⃝⃝⃝⃝⃝'⃝ ⃝⃝ ⃝⃝⃝⃝⃝ IT

JUMBLE®

Unscramble these six Jumbles, one letter to each square, to form six ordinary words.

RETHOB

HERFIE

MOARRY

YULTIG

GRIFIN

NALTED

WHY IT CAN BE DANGEROUS TO TELL A PERSON A FUNNY STORY.

Print answer here

HE MIGHT ☐☐☐☐☐☐ HIS ☐☐☐☐ ☐☐☐

165

JUMBLE®

Unscramble these six Jumbles, one letter
to each square, to form six ordinary words.

BRUNAU

TAJECK

DRUSAB

ENCOSH

GUTHAN

BRUZZE

WHAT THAT EXPERT
MASSEUR LEFT.

Now arrange the circled letters
to form the surprise answer, as
suggested by the above cartoon.

*Print answer
here* NO

JUMBLE®

Unscramble these six Jumbles, one letter to each square, to form six ordinary words.

DOLBIE

INGEEN

PHASIM

CLINEP

TURGED

CATCEN

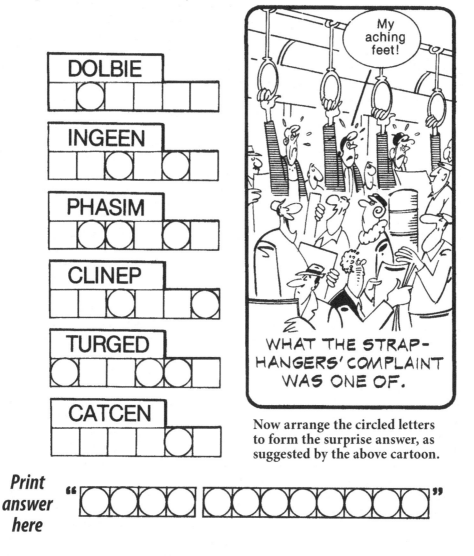

My aching feet!

WHAT THE STRAP-HANGERS' COMPLAINT WAS ONE OF.

Now arrange the circled letters to form the surprise answer, as suggested by the above cartoon.

Print answer here " ⬡⬡⬡⬡⬡ ⬡⬡⬡⬡⬡⬡⬡⬡ "

JUMBLE®

Unscramble these six Jumbles, one letter
to each square, to form six ordinary words.

ROCCUN

GISTED

LAFFEB

COSHOL

MACPIT

YORMME

How about it,
Daddy-o?

WHAT A YOUNG
MAN WHO ASKS FOR
DAUGHTER'S HAND
SOMETIMES GETS.

Now arrange the circled letters
to form the surprise answer, as
suggested by the above cartoon.

**Print
answer
here**

◯◯◯◯◯◯'◯ ◯◯◯◯

JUMBLE®

Unscramble these six Jumbles, one letter to each square, to form six ordinary words.

NALIFE

TOFFES

ENBARN

PEESLY

CLOAJE

TOWPUN

Some people go for anything

A POLITICAL CANDIDATE USUALLY "STANDS" FOR THIS.

Now arrange the circled letters to form the surprise answer, as suggested by the above cartoon.

Print answer here

WHAT THE ⭕⭕⭕⭕⭕⭕ WILL "⭕⭕⭕⭕" FOR

JUMBLE®

Unscramble these six Jumbles, one letter
to each square, to form six ordinary words.

YOLFEN

RUQRAY

NEUQUI

POOSUR

GEDUBB

POMLEY

ONE PLACE
WHERE YOU'RE
SURE TO FIND
A HELPING HAND.

Now arrange the circled letters
to form the surprise answer, as
suggested by the above cartoon.

Print
answer
here

AT
THE

JUMBLE ®

Unscramble these six Jumbles, one letter
to each square, to form six ordinary words.

ZIGAHN

DUBACT

NIPICC

ZIEFER

VARMEL

ROTTAH

Why did
you put
holes in
your
umbrella?

So I can see
whether it's
stopped
raining

HE'S SO DUMB THAT
WHEN HE GETS A
BRAINSTORM IT'S
NOTHING BUT THIS.

Now arrange the circled letters
to form the surprise answer, as
suggested by the above cartoon.

**Print answer
here**

JUMBLE®

Unscramble these six Jumbles, one letter
to each square, to form six ordinary words.

DAREPE

UNMAUT

LIGGEG

PLERTI

MOCHER

GRIBED

He ought
to retire

THE COMEDIAN COULD
NO LONGER FIND
AUDIENCES, BECAUSE
EVERYONE WHO HEARD
HIS JOKES DID THIS.

Now arrange the circled letters
to form the surprise answer, as
suggested by the above cartoon.

Print answer here

JUMBLE®

Unscramble these six Jumbles, one letter to each square, to form six ordinary words.

LASSIA

WROFUR

CAPNUK

OPTECK

RAZABA

MADENT

How about cake?

NO

NO

Ice cream?

NO NO

Candy?

WHAT THE EXACTING DIETICIAN WAS DETERMINED TO DO WITH HER OVERWEIGHT PATIENTS.

Now arrange the circled letters to form the surprise answer, as suggested by the above cartoon.

Print answer here ◯◯◯ THEM ◯◯◯◯ TO ◯◯◯◯

173

JUMBLE

Unscramble these six Jumbles, one letter
to each square, to form six ordinary words.

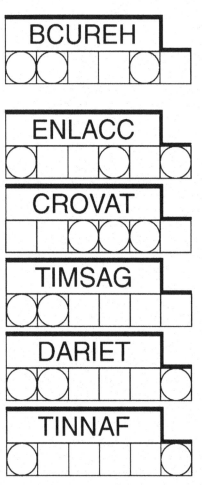

BCUREH

ENLACC

CROVAT

TIMSAG

DARIET

TINNAF

This should
help you watch
your items.

Now, I can
keep an
eye on the
whole
store.

THE FASHION BOUTIQUE
HAD A SHOPLIFTING
PROBLEM, SO THEY
INSTALLED ----

Now arrange the circled letters
to form the surprise answer, as
suggested by the above cartoon.

Print answer here

"◯◯◯◯◯◯◯" - ◯◯◯◯◯◯◯ ◯◯

JUMBLE®

Unscramble these six Jumbles, one letter
to each square, to form six ordinary words.

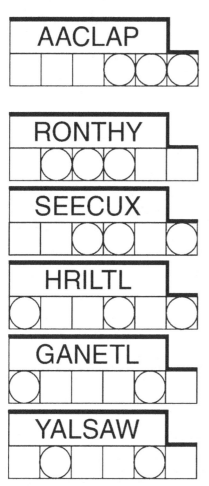

AACLAP

RONTHY

SEECUX

HRILTL

GANETL

YALSAW

Better luck next
season, fellas.

I can't
beleive he
grabbed
that.

AFTER HE SCORED THE
WINNING TOUCHDOWN, THE
WIDE RECEIVER TOLD HIS
OPPONENTS ----

Now arrange the circled letters
to form the surprise answer, as
suggested by the above cartoon.

Print answer here

◯'◯◯ ◯◯◯◯◯ ◯◯◯ ◯◯◯◯◯

JUMBLE®

Unscramble these six Jumbles, one letter
to each square, to form six ordinary words.

CIPTAM

HAACTT

EKCLOT

KAHENS

CITFEN

CICNLI

I can't believe I left the gear at home.

We can use the cork as a bobber, then untangle the old line. While I sharpen the old hook, you dig up some worms.

THE FISHERMEN DIDN'T HAVE
FISHING POLES AND THEY
LACKED PROPER BAIT,
SO IT WAS ---

Now arrange the circled letters
to form the surprise answer, as
suggested by the above cartoon.

Print answer here

JUMBLE®

Unscramble these six Jumbles, one letter
to each square, to form six ordinary words.

SOPSIG

NIVHAS

XIFETA

RALYEN

TOMINO

SISNTI

Just do what
Jesse says, and
you'll do great.

Make sure you
use a new towel
with each car.
Also, wipe in a
clockwise
direction.

THE BEST EMPLOYEE
AT THE CAR WASH
WAS A ---

Now arrange the circled letters
to form the surprise answer, as
suggested by the above cartoon.

Print answer here

JUMBLE®

Unscramble these six Jumbles, one letter to each square, to form six ordinary words.

WDOTAR

SAGINS

GONELU

DULCED

HAYWON

TGRINS

This is the biggest bridal party I've ever seen.

The dresses never seem to end.

THE SEAMSTRESS MADE ONE DRESS ... THEN ANOTHER ... THEN ANOTHER ---

Now arrange the circled letters to form the surprise answer, as suggested by the above cartoon.

Print answer here

◯◯◯ " ◯◯◯ " ◯◯ , ◯◯◯ " ◯◯◯ " ◯◯

JUMBLE®

Unscramble these six Jumbles, one letter
to each square, to form six ordinary words.

BOLLAG

EVIDAC

THEKSC

PENLUG

DINDHE

TONCOT

The Sand Bar

It's like a feeding frenzy in here.

Here's your Blue Lagoon.

THE NEW UNDERSEA BAR
WAS DOING WELL. IT WAS
SO CROWDED WITH FISH
THAT IT WAS ----

Now arrange the circled letters
to form the surprise answer, as
suggested by the above cartoon.

Print answer here

179

JUMBLE®

Unscramble these six Jumbles, one letter
to each square, to form six ordinary words.

TNEETX

RUBUNA

FANELI

MATTOO

GONIRI

SULVIA

RUFF FARMS

This place is great!
It's been in the
same family for
years.

I love our home.
The food and pasture
are great.

HORSES AT THIS FARM
WERE HAPPY AND GOT
ALONG WELL, THANKS IN
PART TO IT BEING A ----

Now arrange the circled letters
to form the surprise answer, as
suggested by the above cartoon.

Print answer here

Unscramble these six Jumbles, one letter
to each square, to form six ordinary words.

CNOOHH

TAUDSJ

TRWHTA

NRREOY

CISELK

SIPEMO

I've never seen someone polish a car so well.

You're not so bad yourself.

THE CAR WASH EMPLOYEE
WAS SMITTEN WITH HIS
NEW COWORKER AND
INSTANTLY ---

Now arrange the circled letters
to form the surprise answer, as
suggested by the above cartoon.

Print answer here

JUMBLE®

Unscramble these six Jumbles, one letter
to each square, to form six ordinary words.

NYCARK

FONEDF

VELOVE

NUBINO

UNBYTO

TRRWIE

There's no way we're naming this after you! I found it!

You thought it was a pile of rocks!

WHO WOULD BE GETTING CREDIT FOR FINDING THE FOSSILIZED DINOSAUR SKELETON WAS A – – –

Now arrange the circled letters
to form the surprise answer, as
suggested by the above cartoon.

Print answer here

182

JUMBLE®

Unscramble these six Jumbles, one letter
to each square, to form six ordinary words.

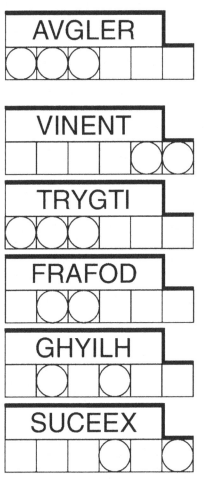

AVGLER

VINENT

TRYGTI

FRAFOD

GHYILH

SUCEEX

Your hubby
is such a
great dad.

Junior
worships
him.

Remember,
1 ten = 10 ones.
Now calculate how
many ones you
can make from 8
tens. Count by
tens.

I get it! Eight tens
equal 80 ones.

WHEN HE SHOWED HIS SON
HOW TO SOLVE MATH
PROBLEMS, THE DAD WAS ---

Now arrange the circled letters
to form the surprise answer, as
suggested by the above cartoon.

Print answer here

Answers

1. **Jumbles:** HOIST ENSUE CEMENT MUSLIN
   Answer: This tells you what the fare is—THE MENU

2. **Jumbles:** ELATE SAUTE WHINNY HOOKED
   Answer: What a gal who's on her toes keeps—
   AWAY FROM HEELS

3. **Jumbles:** IDIOM BELLE FEDORA LOUNGE
   Answer: What he wished he had worn on a blind date—
   A BLINDFOLD

4. **Jumbles:** EJECT SAHIB KILLER BELONG
   Answer: Some veteran gardeners might find this the hardest
   thing to raise—THEIR KNEES

5. **Jumbles:** WALTZ STOKE THIRTY PILLAR
   Answer: A figure in the middle of a figure—THE WAIST

6. **Jumbles:** TITLE AGONY GAINED EMBODY
   Answer: What girls who play hard to get sometimes never do—
   GET GOT

7. **Jumbles:** NOTCH ROUSE CAUCUS AMOEBA
   Answer: Have an unhappy effect on some people with pluck—
   THORNS

8. **Jumbles:** GORGE MINUS DELUXE IMPACT
   Answer: How witch doctors keep fit—THEY "EXORCISE"

9. **Jumbles:** COUGH MOUNTS BAKING INFLUX
   Answer: Some girls break dates by doing this—
   GOING OUT WITH THEM

10. **Jumbles:** POACH OUTDO CORRAL ENSIGN
    Answer: What yes-men do—STOOP TO CONCUR

11. **Jumbles:** CEASE AGATE CAMPUS DRIVEL
    Answer: Could be the price of hiring a private guide to take you
    mountain climbing—STEEP

12. **Jumbles:** MAKER FRANC LOTION HAMPER
    Answer: What a Crimean became after receiving his citizenship
    papers—"AMERICAN"

13. **Jumbles:** TANGY QUEER CARBON PIRATE
    Answer: Where an unemployed person might find an
    opening—AT THE ENTRANCE

14. **Jumbles:** BRIBE WHOOP SIZZLE CAMPER
    Answer: What the policewoman who entered the beauty
    contest was expected to do—COP A PRIZE

15. **Jumbles:** WHILE VILLA CURFEW FRIGID
    Answer: Not many are to be seen in the café window—"A FEW"

16. **Jumbles:** AVAIL EMPTY JINGLE OPPOSE
    Answer: Could be the result of a toss-up—what you should
    wear—"TAILS"

17. **Jumbles:** WHOSE PIOUS TOTTER BUCKET
    Answer: What cuts in medical care usually call for—STITCHES

18. **Jumbles:** KNIFE FAVOR DETACH HOOKED
    Answer: The parent—ends up—paying it—"RENT"

19. **Jumbles:** THICK SQUAW IMBIBE HARROW
    Answer: Could be a question of price—HOW MUCH?

20. **Jumbles:** SUEDE NOVEL BALSAM ELICIT
    Answer: What hot music does to people with "square" tastes—
    LEAVES THEM COLD

21. **Jumbles:** LIVEN SCARY WEASEL BAMBOO
    Answer: A name is—confused—when one can't remember—
    "AMNESIA"

22. **Jumbles:** CAMEO JUMPY ELIXIR TALKER
    Answer: What the student beautician had to take—
    A MAKE-UP EXAM

23. **Jumbles:** CRAZE DOGMA BANANA WAITER
    Answer: What the desert rat said to his pal—
    WATER WE GONNA DO?

24. **Jumbles:** UPPER WRATH CANNED BEWAIL
    Answer: Did the lawyer do his best in court?—HE "TRIED"

25. **Jumbles:** PROVE USURY TAMPER HORROR
    Answer: What his stories had lots of—"RYE" HUMOR

26. **Jumbles:** DEITY HASTY BANNER AWEIGH
    Answer: What they had to do when the clock collector passed
    away—WIND UP HIS ESTATE

27. **Jumbles:** GLADE MACAW PARLOR NOBODY
    Answer: Try this diet if you want to become a tightrope
    walker—"BALANCED"

28. **Jumbles:** AGONY TEMPO INVENT ATOMIC
    Answer: What the trumpet player's girlfriend accused him of
    doing—TOOT-TIMING HER

29. **Jumbles:** FORTY ETUDE DRAGON GOVERN
    Answer: What he said when asked whether he had liked
    college—TO A "DEGREE"

30. **Jumbles:** ANNOY DOUGH SOCIAL INJURY
    Answer: Might describe some things done in Congress—
    "INCONGRUOUS"

31. **Jumbles:** TRILL DADDY HALLOW GADFLY
    Answer: Sounds like a pretty good distance on the golf
    course—A "FAIR WAY"

32. **Jumbles:** HAIRY DELVE EXPOSE CROUCH
    Answer: "Here's how!"—in the kitchen—RECIPE

33. **Jumbles:** DOILY VALVE WEEVIL CANINE
    Answer: Words heard during a honeymoon—"I LOVE VIEW"

34. **Jumbles:** ROACH DALLY CALIPH EMERGE
    Answer: Represents the country—on paper, at least—A MAP

35. **Jumbles:** PATCH LURID WEAKEN ENTIRE
    Answer: What a model may be when under a strain—"DRAWN"

36. **Jumbles:** JADED RANCH ADMIRE STUPID
    Answer: How to construct an "industry" out of nudity—
    ADD S AND R

37. **Jumbles:** AGILE MOUSE SPLICE ZINNIA
    Answer: What a good clothing salesman does with a new
    customer—SIZES HIM UP

38. **Jumbles:** TWILL UNITY BEHALF JUGGLE
    Answer: What they made when there was a power failure—
    LIGHT OF IT

39. **Jumbles:** WEARY LOFTY SWERVE INBORN
    Answer: For these opera singers—could be no rest—"TENORS"

40. **Jumbles:** TOPAZ LANKY AGENDA FOMENT
    Answer: Add something to a "No," and it might be yes—
    A "NO-D"

41. **Jumbles:** FOAMY KINKY NUTRIA CORNEA
    Answer: Doesn't sound like preparation for war when they arm
    thus—"IN ARM" (arm in arm)

42. **Jumbles:** LLAMA ASSAY FLAUNT HECKLE
    Answer: What little babies sometimes indulge in—"SMALL" TALK

43. **Jumbles:** LOWLY SHEAF GALLEY FINITE
    Answer: A kind of "art" you might be surprised to find in a
    moving picture—"STILL LIFE"

44. **Jumbles:** TOXIN ELATE FALTER MIDDAY
    Answer: If an alteration is required, you should get it from
    this—A "NEAT TAILOR"

45. **Jumbles:** KHAKI DUMPY UNSEAT ENTITY
    Answer: What the captain of the ark said he had no shortage
    of—"MATES"

46. **Jumbles:** GAMUT WELSH UPHELD SQUALL
    Answer: A very fine wood was in evidence—SAWDUST

47. **Jumbles:** TAWNY KEYED COUGAR BENIGN
    Answer: "I have a certain importance when angry!"—"I-RATE"

48. **Jumbles:** SWASH OFTEN GOLFER FAULTY
    Answer: Generally left at the sink—THE HOT WATER

49. **Jumbles:** FACET CLUCK BOBBIN GENTRY
Answer: Inclined to be on the thin side—LEAN

50. **Jumbles:** REARM ABBOT JUMBLE ADVICE
Answer: A bridge foundation that may collapse—A CARD TABLE

51. **Jumbles:** WOVEN DINER AVOWAL BRIDLE
Answer: How the plumber felt after a hard day's work—"DRAINED"

52. **Jumbles:** MANLY ROUSE EXTANT OPIATE
Answer: What mixing up trains might be for a traveler—A "STRAIN"

53. **Jumbles:** BRINY OXIDE GOPHER EFFIGY
Answer: What the boss's son was, naturally—"FIRE-PROOF"

54. **Jumbles:** FUDGE TULLE RANCOR PAYING
Answer: What some guys who never seem to get around to marrying just get—"AROUND"

55. **Jumbles:** HAVOC GRAIN INJECT SURELY
Answer: What a talkative barber might do—GET IN YOUR HAIR

56. **Jumbles:** HOUSE AFIRE GENTRY KIDNAP
Answer: What the chairman of the mathematics department was called—THE FIGUREHEAD

57. **Jumbles:** AUGUR TOOTH WINTRY RACIAL
Answer: What the patient said when his doctor told him to diet—WHAT COLOR?

58. **Jumbles:** ICILY CRACK MADMAN GYRATE
Answer: When they took that tropical vacation, they apparently were saving their money for this—A RAINY DAY

59. **Jumbles:** FETCH HITCH CATTLE PARODY
Answer: What they called the team's psychiatrist—THE "HEAD" COACH

60. **Jumbles:** CREEL MACAW SULTRY FEWEST
Answer: Alcohol will preserve almost everything except this—SECRETS

61. **Jumbles:** KNACK TULIP NOZZLE CASHEW
Answer: What some people do at sneak previews—SNEAK OUT

62. **Jumbles:** KEYED CURIO VESTRY CALLOW
Answer: What you can expect a smart cookie to be—A WISE "CRACKER"

63. **Jumbles:** BOOTY ODIUM TOTTER GYPSUM
Answer: If it's a Dracula whom you meet on the street, he'll sure know how to do this—PUT THE BITE ON YOU

64. **Jumbles:** SUITE HASTY MARKUP STIGMA
Answer: What a hula dance is—A SHAKE IN THE GRASS

65. **Jumbles:** APART POACH PAYOFF CHEERY
Answer: What they called the police officers' annual shindig—THE "COP HOP"

66. **Jumbles:** APRON HANDY ENZYME BAZAAR
Answer: What the picnickers were—"HAMPERED"

67. **Jumbles:** ONION CHANT GASKET NESTLE
Answer: Where there's smoke—SHE'S COOKING

68. **Jumbles:** IMBUE SKULL UNCLAD SYMBOL
Answer: What the guy whose shoes squeaked must have had—MUSIC IN HIS "SOLE"

69. **Jumbles:** JETTY RAINY ADROIT CLEAVE
Answer: What the ballerina insisted that her partner do—"TOE" THE LINE

70. **Jumbles:** JOINT CUBIC COERCE DISMAY
Answer: There's plenty of this when a man doesn't pay alimony—ACRIMONY

71. **Jumbles:** HAVEN TWEAK MYOPIC WAYLAY
Answer: The boss always came in early to see this—WHO CAME IN LATE

72. **Jumbles:** BARON TWICE WEDGED LAWFUL
Answer: What that incompetent political seemed to live by—THE LAW OF THE "BUNGLE"

73. **Jumbles:** TESTY ABIDE ELIXIR LACING
Answer: In order to select the finest wine, examine this—THE BEST-CELLAR LIST

74. **Jumbles:** NUDGE CRANK VARIED CAVORT
Answer: When you're in it, you never know—IGNORANCE

75. **Jumbles:** BRAVE LOONY VASSAL PUMICE
Answer: What the polite crook used when he held up the public library—A SILENCER

76. **Jumbles:** BELIE TRULY HAWKER LEVITY
Answer: Some people who think they're "in the swim" are just this—ALL WET

77. **Jumbles:** GUIDE WOVEN ENTITY CLOVEN
Answer: "My husband found a new position"—LYING DOWN

78. **Jumbles:** BUSHY SCARY HANDED EROTIC
Answer: What he apparently took in order to learn to drive—A "CRASH" COURSE

79. **Jumbles:** FUZZY SKULK FEDORA PETITE
Answer: He said he would love her for this—THE REST OF HIS "DAZE"

80. **Jumbles:** BERYL GUMMY GRAVEN PLOVER
Answer: How to acquire a huge vocabulary—MARRY ONE

81. **Jumbles:** CROWN AFTER TRENDY FORAGE
Answer: The rodent who lived in the big city was growing tired of the—RAT RACE

82. **Jumbles:** BLURB FOGGY FEEBLE ABSORB
Answer: When the delectable turkey was put on the table, everyone was anxious to—GOBBLE GOBBLE

83. **Jumbles:** SCARF UNITY EXOTIC REVIVE
Answer: The railroad sold off their older surplus boxcars because they were—"EX-TRAIN-EOUS"

84. **Jumbles:** WORLD SUNNY INTACT GIGGLE
Answer: When the plant nursery bought more land, they were this on their competition —GAINING GROUND

85. **Jumbles:** FLOCK VENUE LESSON GERBIL
Answer: The tennis balls at the courts were—SELF-SERVE

86. **Jumbles:** EAGLE OOMPH NIBBLE SKIMPY
Answer: To close deals, a good real estate salesperson needs a—"SELL" PHONE

87. **Jumbles:** ROBOT ISSUE SMELLY ABACUS
Answer: When his son said he was starting a rock band, it wasn't—MUSIC TO HIS EARS

88. **Jumbles:** LEVEL ABATE OPENLY WIZARD
Answer: They wanted an affordable home, but the one they looked at didn't—"ABODE" WELL

89. **Jumbles:** SINGE DOUSE TRUDGE LETTER
Answer: It was time to close her bakery for the day after the customers had—"DESSERTED" IT

90. **Jumbles:** DRANK OUTDO SHREWD IGUANA
Answer: The kids on the carnival's carousel were—HORSING AROUND

91. **Jumbles:** SNIFF NINTH FICKLE GAGGLE
Answer: After watching his opponent make shot after shot, he was getting a—SINKING FEELING

92. **Jumbles:** AFTER TOKEN ORIOLE PEOPLE
Answer: Customers arrived at the new shoe store—ON FOOT

93. **Jumbles:** TENTH ODDLY SPRAWL APIECE
Answer: The palm reader saved a lot of money, and now retirement was—CLOSE AT HAND

94. **Jumbles:** MAUVE BRING TEMPLE MAYHEM
Answer: The leprechaun who grew his own shamrocks had a—GREEN THUMB

95. **Jumbles:** LATCH LINER MASCOT ALLEGE
Answer: He erased the formula from the chalkboard to start over with a—CLEAN SLATE

96. **Jumbles:** PERCH HAVOC FORBID SPRUCE
Answer: In his off-time, Sleepy Hollow's horseman worked in a restaurant as the—HEAD CHEF

97. Jumbles: BOGUS TOXIN FROSTY PIRACY
Answer: With the success of the 707, the Boeing Company had—SOARING PROFITS

98. Jumbles: BUGGY LEAKY ENTICE FUTURE
Answer: He wasn't positive he had food poisoning, but he had a—GUT FEELING

99. Jumbles: DIVOT SEEDY GALAXY EMBLEM
Answer: The 40-year-old knights in the 1300s had—MIDDLE-AGES

100. Jumbles: ELOPE TIGER GATHER ANNUAL
Answer: They disagreed about which weapon was best and continued to—ARGUE THE POINT

101. Jumbles: BOXER EMPTY ALPACA SOCKET
Answer: We can never truly compensate those who fought for our country, but we can—PAY RESPECT

102. Jumbles: PARTY POISE RIPPLE LOCKET
Answer: When Edmund Hillary and Tenzing Norgay reached Everest's peak, it was a—TOP STORY

103. Jumbles: ASKED SUSHI DOCKET CHATTY
Answer: The locksmith had great customer service, which he considered to be a—KEY TO SUCCESS

104. Jumbles: NIPPY EAGLE CLOSET HEALTH
Answer: When their kids and pets crawled into bed with them, they were able to—SLEEP TIGHT

105. Jumbles: PURGE HEAVY POETIC TANDEM
Answer: The popular car model's price was being—DRIVEN UP

106. Jumbles: GIANT KUDOS CHANCE REVOLT
Answer: When they finished high school, he complimented them all by saying—"CONGRADULATIONS"

107. Jumbles: HATCH EVOKE GROUND PASTRY
Answer: The scuba-diving philosopher had—DEEP THOUGHTS

108. Jumbles: JUDGE HABIT BUNDLE DOLLAR
Answer: They would pilot the first Boeing 747 test flight now that they'd—LANDED THE JOB

109. Jumbles: TRUNK ABOUT STOCKY FACTOR
Answer: The sprinter was losing races and needed to train harder to get his career—BACK ON TRACK

110. Jumbles: ONION HOIST OUTLAW DAWNED
Answer: When the dentist and the carpenter argued about the construction, they fought—TOOTH AND NAIL

111. Jumbles: SLANT HOUSE VIABLE INFANT
Answer: The squirrel was able to summarize his love of pecans, cashews, almonds—IN A NUTSHELL

112. Jumbles: OFTEN ALIAS NEPHEW SAILOR
Answer: The tired dogs turned the couch into a—SLEEPER SOFA

113. Jumbles: MIMIC GUAVA WANTED GUITAR
Answer: When is a dog's tail not a tail? When it's a—"WAGGIN'"

114. Jumbles: ERUPT SHAME HAIRDO ADRIFT
Answer: Sleepy Hollow's Horseman needed to get to New York City, so he—HEADED SOUTH

115. Jumbles: IVORY LOBBY GEYSER ADJOIN
Answer: For them, saying goodbye took—SO LONG

116. Jumbles: CAGEY RODEO DIVINE PUCKER
Answer: The rooster would have to wait to eat because there was a—PECKING ORDER

117. Jumbles: PHONY HELLO FIDDLE TAXING
Answer: After landing in Hawaii, they got the—"LEI" OF THE LAND

118. Jumbles: MACAW SCARF HARBOR EQUITY
Answer: She loved making dresses by hand—"SEW" MUCH

119. Jumbles: LOGIC CONGA DONKEY JUNIOR
Answer: She knew the difference between stratus, cirrus and cumulus and was—ON CLOUD NINE

120. Jumbles: CROON PILOT BOTHER FABRIC
Answer: Before Pete Rose took over as the all-time hit leader, he had to—"TIE" COBB

121. Jumbles: JUICY UPEND WOBBLE GYRATE
Answer: The barber who cut the Beatles' hair in 1963 did a—BANG-UP JOB

122. Jumbles: AGENT BUNCH NEURON WICKET
Answer: The spiders thought their kids were spending too much time—ON THE WEB

123. Jumbles: GAUDY COURT KISSED THEORY
Answer: The struggling young golfer wanted to quit, but her coach recommended she—STAY THE COURSE

124. Jumbles: PANSY POOCH WILDLY NORMAL
Answer: She wanted to borrow the scissors, but her sister was being—SNIPPY

125. Jumbles: MINCE QUACK ROOKIE BUREAU
Answer: The baby delivered at 30,000 feet was—AIRBORNE

126. Jumbles: KNACK GUARD CACTUS MINGLE
Answer: The tennis player couldn't find his equipment in the closet and was—MAKING A RACKET

127. Jumbles: PUTTY DOUSE COGNAC NIMBLE
Answer: When the couple tried out their new furniture while watching TV, they watched a—SITCOM

128. Jumbles: GROVE CLOUT DOODLE SCRIPT
Answer: He told his wife there wouldn't be a long line, but he—STOOD CORRECTED

129. Jumbles: LOWLY ADOPT FOURTH PLAGUE
Answer: When elevators in buildings started to become popular, people were—FLOORED

130. Jumbles: LUNGE WELSH CATNIP FORMAL
Answer: When the royal marine mammals had a baby boy, he was the—PRINCE OF "WHALES"

131. Jumbles: IMAGE GLORY HYPHEN SPRAWL
Answer: The bowlers who started placing bets were—HIGH ROLLERS

132. Jumbles: POUCH IRONY PILLAR HIGHLY
Answer: When the hula dancers entertained the sailors, the sailors said—HIP HIP HOORAY

133. Jumbles: CROSS RELIC DEVOUR CAMPUS
Answer: The classic vinyl albums were selling for—RECORD PRICES

134. Jumbles: FLOOD LUCKY SLOWLY KITTEN
Answer: To get more customers, the locksmith set up a—"KEY-OSK"

135. Jumbles: ABATE TROLL SPLASH ATTEST
Answer: When they built the new roundabout, they pulled out—ALL THE STOPS

136. Jumbles: USHER YIELD PLUNGE ODDEST
Answer: He dozed off listening to music on his headphones, and was able to—SLEEP SOUNDLY

137. Jumbles: RIGOR GRAPH OUTWIT UPDATE
Answer: The nursery that sold bamboo was experiencing—RAPID GROWTH

138. Jumbles: USURP GOURD MANNER UNWISE
Answer: She wanted her daughter to clean her room and wasn't—MESSING AROUND

139. Jumbles: POLKA FLUID MANAGE OUTING
Answer: To cover the opening of the new shoe store, the TV news crew needed—FOOTAGE

140. Jumbles: FOCAL ROBOT FOLLOW TACKLE
Answer: Preparing for the Labor Day cookout was—A LOT OF WORK

141. Jumbles: MOOSE INPUT NIBBLE WARMLY
Answer: The wheel hadn't quite been invented, but the wheels—WERE IN MOTION

142. Jumbles: GRANT HONOR INSIST RODENT
Answer: It's easy to add zero plus zero because there's—NOTHING TO IT

143. **Jumbles:** WALTZ ELECT FINISH ELEVEN
Answer: After her divorce, she moved, wanting a—
NEW LEASE ON LIFE

144. **Jumbles:** BOTCH WINCE BOTANY WEEKLY
Answer: The baseball team's winning streak continued—
"WON" BY "WON"

145. **Jumbles:** MUDDY AROSE SHRINK BURLAP
Answer: Male models with successful careers are—
PAID HANDSOMELY

146. **Jumbles:** RAZOR FAITH ROCKET MEMORY
Answer: After realizing how much corn he had for sale, the
farmer was grinning—FROM EAR TO EAR

147. **Jumbles:** SCARF PUPIL GENTLY SCROLL
Answer: The laundromat that installed exercise equipment
featured—SPIN CYCLES

148. **Jumbles:** BUILD COMIC FALLEN RADIUS
Answer: When the Jumble creators realized they'd forgotten to
make a puzzle, they—SCRAMBLED

149. **Jumbles:** PROXY BANJO SPEEDY WICKED
Answer: When audiences watched this 1975 film about a great
white shark, their—JAWS DROPPED

150. **Jumbles:** SCOUT ADOPT GENDER PULLEY
Answer: The landlord reduced the young couple's rent, saying it
was the—"LEASE" SHE COULD DO

151. **Jumbles:** BISON METAL FUMBLE PROVEN
Answer: The math teacher had taught multiplication a—
NUMBER OF TIMES

152. **Jumbles:** SORRY BERRY POETIC DEBATE
Answer: The clever Hungarian exterminator named his new
company—"BOOT-A-PEST"

153. **Jumbles:** COVET TEMPT SHIFTY INFORM
Answer: The new discount retailer's customers had great
deals— IN STORE FOR THEM

154. **Jumbles:** VALID CREPT SURELY BICEPS
Answer: One way to avoid heart surgery is to exercise and eat
well. Then you can—BYPASS IT

155. **Jumbles:** SHINY GAVEL BITTER REGRET
Answer: The Alaskan fishing-boat captain was disoriented and
needed to get his—"BERING STRAIT"

156. **Jumbles:** GOING ODDLY DEFIED SCENIC
Answer: The get information before cutting hair, the salon
owner did—"DO" DILIGENCE

157. **Jumbles:** MOUND YEAST WILLOW GASKET
Answer: The fashion designer retired at the top of her career so
that she could—GO OUT IN STYLE

158. **Jumbles:** HUTCH EMCEE SALARY JUSTLY
Answer: When the farmer greeted the horses at feeding time, he
said—"HAY" THERE

159. **Jumbles:** KOALA GRILL MIFFED RELENT
Answer: Kong had trouble finding a meal that was—
FIT FOR A KING

160. **Jumbles:** UNION VISTA KEEPER GARLIC
Answer: To help the young hunting dog learn, the experienced
hunting dog—GAVE POINTERS

161. **Jumbles:** PUSHER GIGGLE INDUCE TURBAN COMPLY DONKEY
Answer: Why the horse galloped over the hill—
HE COULDN'T GO UNDER IT

162. **Jumbles:** BOTHER HEIFER ARMORY GUILTY FIRING DENTAL
Answer: Why it can be dangerous to tell a person a funny
story—HE MIGHT LAUGH HIS HEAD OFF

163. **Jumbles:** AUBURN JACKET ABSURD CHOSEN NAUGHT BUZZER
Answer: What that expert masseur left—NO STERN UNTONED

164. **Jumbles:** BOILED ENGINE MISHAP PENCIL TRUDGE ACCENT
Answer: What the straphangers' complaint was one of—"LONG
STANDING"

165. **Jumbles:** CONCUR DIGEST BAFFLE SCHOOL IMPACT MEMORY
Answer: What a young man who asks for daughter's hand
sometimes gets—FATHER'S FOOT

166. **Jumbles:** FINALE OFFSET BANNER SLEEPY CAJOLE UPTOWN
Answer: A political candidate usually "stands" for this—
WHAT THE PEOPLE WILL "FALL" FOR

167. **Jumbles:** FELONY QUARRY UNIQUE POROUS BEDBUG EMPLOY
Answer: One place where you're sure to find a helping hand—
AT THE END OF YOUR ARM

168. **Jumbles:** HAZING ABDUCT PICNIC FRIEZE MARVEL THROAT
Answer: He's so dumb that when he gets a brainstorm it's
nothing but this—A DRIZZLE

169. **Jumbles:** PARADRE AUTUMN GIGGLE TRIPLE CHROME BRIDGE
Answer: The comedian could no longer find audiences, because
everyone who heard his jokes did this—DIED LAUGHING

170. **Jumbles:** ASSAIL FURROW UNPACK POCKET BAZAAR TANDEM
Answer: What the exacting dietician was determined to do with
her overweight patients—CUT THEM DOWN TO SIZE

171. **Jumbles:** CHERUB CANCEL CAVORT STIGMA TIRADE INFANT
Answer: The fashion boutique had a shoplifting problem, so
they installed—"CLOTHES"-CIRCUIT TV

172. **Jumbles:** ALPACA THORNY EXCUSE THRILL TANGLE ALWAYS
Answer: After he scored the winning touchdown, the wide
receiver told his opponents—I'LL CATCH YOU LATER

173. **Jumbles:** IMPACT ATTACH LOCKET SHAKEN INFECT CLINIC
Answer: The fishermen didn't have fishing poles and they lacked
proper bait, so it was—CATCH-AS-CATCH-CAN

174. **Jumbles:** GOSSIP VANISH FIXATE NEARLY MOTION INSIST
Answer: The best employee at the car wash was a —SHINING
EXAMPLE

175. **Jumbles:** TOWARD ASSIGN LOUNGE CUDDLE ANYHOW STRING
Answer: The seamstress made one dress…then another…then
another—AND "SEW" ON, AND "SEW" ON

176. **Jumbles:** GLOBAL ADVICE SKETCH PLUNGE HIDDEN COTTON
Answer: The new undersea bar was doing well. It was so
crowded with fish that it was—PACKED TO THE GILLS

177. **Jumbles:** EXTENT AUBURN FINALE TOMATO ORIGINAL VISUAL
Answer: Horses at this farm were happy and got along well,
thanks in part to it being a—STABLE ENVIRONMENT

178. **Jumbles:** HONCHO ADJUST THWART ORNERY SICKLE IMPOSE
Answer: The car wash employee was smitten with his new
coworker and instantly—TOOK A SHINE TO HER

179. **Jumbles:** CRANKY OFFEND EVOLVE BUNION BOUNTY WRITER
Answer: Who would be getting credit for finding the fossilized
dinosaur skeleton was a—BONE OF CONTENTION

180. **Jumbles:** GRAVEL INVENT GRITTY AFFORD HIGHLY EXCUSE
Answer: When he showed his son how to solve math problems,
the dad was—FATHER FIGURING

187

Need More Jumbles®?

Jumble® Books

More than 175 puzzles each!

Cowboy Jumble®
$9.95 • ISBN: 978-1-62937-355-3

Jammin' Jumble®
$9.95 • ISBN: 1-57243-844-4

Java Jumble®
$9.95 • ISBN: 978-1-60078-415-6

Jazzy Jumble®
$9.95 • ISBN: 978-1-57243-962-7

Jet Set Jumble®
$9.95 • ISBN: 978-1-60078-353-1

Joyful Jumble®
$9.95 • ISBN: 978-1-60078-079-0

Juke Joint Jumble®
$9.95 • ISBN: 978-1-60078-295-4

Jumble® Anniversary
$10.95 • ISBN: 987-1-62937-734-6

Jumble® at Work
$9.95 • ISBN: 1-57243-147-4

Jumble® Ballet
$10.95 • ISBN: 978-1-62937-616-5

Jumble® Birthday
$10.95 • ISBN: 978-1-62937-652-3

Jumble® Celebration
$9.95 • ISBN: 978-1-60078-134-6

Jumble® Champion
$10.95 • ISBN: 978-1-62937-870-1

Jumble® Circus
$9.95 • ISBN: 978-1-60078-739-3

Jumble® Cuisine
$10.95 • ISBN: 978-1-62937-735-3

Jumble® Drag Race
$9.95 • ISBN: 978-1-62937-483-3

Jumble® Ever After
$10.95 • ISBN: 978-1-62937-785-8

Jumble® Explorer
$9.95 • ISBN: 978-1-60078-854-3

Jumble® Explosion
$9.95 • ISBN: 978-1-60078-078-3

Jumble® Fever
$9.95 • ISBN: 1-57243-593-3

Jumble® Fiesta
$9.95 • ISBN: 1-57243-626-3

Jumble® Fun
$9.95 • ISBN: 1-57243-379-5

Jumble® Galaxy
$9.95 • ISBN: 978-1-60078-583-2

Jumble® Garden
$10.95 • ISBN: 978-1-62937-653-0

Jumble® Genius
$9.95 • ISBN: 1-57243-896-7

Jumble® Geography
$10.95 • ISBN: 978-1-62937-615-8

Jumble® Getaway
$9.95 • ISBN: 978-1-60078-547-4

Jumble® Gold
$9.95 • ISBN: 978-1-62937-354-6

Jumble® Grab Bag
$9.95 • ISBN: 1-57243-273-X

Jumble® Gymnastics
$9.95 • ISBN: 978-1-62937-306-5

Jumble® Jackpot
$9.95 • ISBN: 1-57243-897-5

Jumble® Jailbreak
$9.95 • ISBN: 978-1-62937-002-6

Jumble® Jambalaya
$9.95 • ISBN: 978-1-60078-294-7

Jumble® Jamboree
$9.95 • ISBN: 1-57243-696-4

Jumble® Jitterbug
$9.95 • ISBN: 978-1-60078-584-9

Jumble® Journey
$9.95 • ISBN: 978-1-62937-549-6

Jumble® Jubilation
$10.95 • ISBN: 978-1-62937-784-1

Jumble® Jubilee
$9.95 • ISBN: 1-57243-231-4

Jumble® Juggernaut
$9.95 • ISBN: 978-1-60078-026-4

Jumble® Junction
$9.95 • ISBN: 1-57243-380-9

Jumble® Jungle
$9.95 • ISBN: 978-1-57243-961-0

Jumble® Kingdom
$9.95 • ISBN: 978-1-62937-079-8

Jumble® Knockout
$9.95 • ISBN: 978-1-62937-078-1

Jumble® Madness
$9.95 • ISBN: 1-892049-24-4

Jumble® Magic
$9.95 • ISBN: 978-1-60078-795-9

Jumble® Marathon
$9.95 • ISBN: 978-1-60078-944-1

Jumble® Neighbor
$10.95 • ISBN: 978-1-62937-845-9

Jumble® Parachute
$10.95 • ISBN: 978-1-62937-548-9

Jumble® Safari
$9.95 • ISBN: 978-1-60078-675-4

Jumble® See & Search
$9.95 • ISBN: 1-57243-549-6

Jumble® See & Search 2
$9.95 • ISBN: 1-57243-734-0

Jumble® Sensation
$9.95 • ISBN: 978-1-60078-548-1

Jumble® Skyscraper
$10.95 • ISBN: 978-1-62937-844-2

Jumble® Surprise
$9.95 • ISBN: 978-1-62937-869-5

Jumble® Symphony
$9.95 • ISBN: 978-1-62937-131-3

Jumble® Theater
$9.95 • ISBN: 978-1-62937-484-03

Jumble® University
$9.95 • ISBN: 978-1-62937-001-9

Jumble® Unleashed
$10.95 • ISBN: 978-1-62937-844-2

Jumble® Vacation
$9.95 • ISBN: 978-1-60078-796-6

Jumble® Wedding
$9.95 • ISBN: 978-1-62937-307-2

Jumble® Workout
$9.95 • ISBN: 978-1-60078-943-4

Jumpin' Jumble®
$9.95 • ISBN: 978-1-60078-027-1

Lunar Jumble®
$9.95 • ISBN: 978-1-60078-853-6

Monster Jumble®
$9.95 • ISBN: 978-1-62937-213-6

Mystic Jumble®
$9.95 • ISBN: 978-1-62937-130-6

Outer Space Jumble®
$9.95 • ISBN: 978-1-60078-416-3

Rainy Day Jumble®
$9.95 • ISBN: 978-1-60078-352-4

Ready, Set, Jumble®
$9.95 • ISBN: 978-1-60078-133-0

Rock 'n' Roll Jumble®
$9.95 • ISBN: 978-1-60078-674-7

Royal Jumble®
$9.95 • ISBN: 978-1-60078-738-6

Sports Jumble®
$9.95 • ISBN: 1-57243-113-X

Summer Fun Jumble®
$9.95 • ISBN: 1-57243-114-8

Touchdown Jumble®
$9.95 • ISBN: 978-1-62937-212-9

Travel Jumble®
$9.95 • ISBN: 1-57243-198-9

TV Jumble®
$9.95 • ISBN: 1-57243-461-9

Oversize Jumble® Books

More than 500 puzzles each!

Generous Jumble®
$19.95 • ISBN: 1-57243-385-X

Giant Jumble®
$19.95 • ISBN: 1-57243-349-3

Gigantic Jumble®
$19.95 • ISBN: 1-57243-426-0

Jumbo Jumble®
$19.95 • ISBN: 1-57243-314-0

The Very Best of Jumble® BrainBusters
$19.95 • ISBN: 1-57243-845-2

Jumble® Crosswords™

More than 175 puzzles each!

More Jumble® Crosswords™
$9.95 • ISBN: 1-57243-386-8

Jumble® Crosswords™ Jackpot
$9.95 • ISBN: 1-57243-615-8

Jumble® Crosswords™ Jamboree
$9.95 • ISBN: 1-57243-787-1

Jumble® BrainBusters™

More than 175 puzzles each!

Jumble® BrainBusters™
$9.95 • ISBN: 1-892049-28-7

Jumble® BrainBusters™ II
$9.95 • ISBN: 1-57243-424-4

Jumble® BrainBusters™ III
$9.95 • ISBN: 1-57243-463-5

Jumble® BrainBusters™ IV
$9.95 • ISBN: 1-57243-489-9

Jumble® BrainBusters™ 5
$9.95 • ISBN: 1-57243-548-8

Jumble® BrainBusters™ Bonanza
$9.95 • ISBN: 1-57243-616-6

Boggle™ BrainBusters™
$9.95 • ISBN: 1-57243-592-5

Boggle™ BrainBusters™ 2
$9.95 • ISBN: 1-57243-788-X

Jumble® BrainBusters™ Junior
$9.95 • ISBN: 1-892049-29-5

Jumble® BrainBusters™ Junior II
$9.95 • ISBN: 1-57243-425-2

Fun in the Sun with Jumble® BrainBusters™
$9.95 • ISBN: 1-57243-733-2